This

Who We Are

This Is
Who We Are

A Scottish history

Kathy Galloway

wild goose
publications   www.**ionabooks**.com

Copyright © 2023 Kathy Galloway

First published 2023 by
Wild Goose Publications
Suite 9, Fairfield
1048 Govan Road, Glasgow G51 4XS, Scotland
A division of Iona Community Trading CIC
Limited Company Reg. No. SC156678
www.ionabooks.com

ISBN 978-1-80432-299-4

Cover map image 'Scotland – southern section' by J Bartholomew
reproduced with the permission of the National Library of Scotland
https://maps.nls.uk/

The publishers gratefully acknowledge the support of the Drummond Trust,
3 Pitt Terrace, Stirling FK8 2EY in producing this book.

Overseas distribution
Australia: Willow Connection Pty Ltd, 1/13 Kell Mather Drive,
Lennox Head NSW 2478
New Zealand: Pleroma, Higginson Street, Otane 4170,
Central Hawkes Bay

Printed in the UK by Page Bros (Norwich) Ltd

Contents

Acknowledgements

This book has been very much a collaborative endeavour. First and foremost, it was inspired by, and depended on, the extensive, exhaustive and ongoing genealogical research into our family history undertaken by my brother Callum Orr over the last twenty years. Eventually I have had to say to him that he must stop sending me new information, or the book will never be finished. This is only the story so far, and new chapters are always coming into being. In addition to sources acknowledged in the Notes, an appendix to the book describes the process and methodology Callum has used in his research, including some of the archives and websites he has consulted.

I am not a historian, only someone with a lifelong interest in the past that we live today. I am therefore greatly indebted to my sister Lesley Orr, who is a historian, and whose advice, knowledge, wisdom and experience, especially in the fields of feminist and ecclesiastical history, I have drawn on continually (and whose library I have raided).

My brother David Orr has been a helpful and thoughtful reader at every stage, and has made valuable contributions, especially in his own area of expertise on housing. We four siblings are the only ones who share our unique DNA and background, and I have been grateful for and enjoyed our ongoing conversations on the book. I have felt always I was writing on behalf of them also.

I want to thank our cousins Marian Hara, Lesley Parrott and David Clelland for photographs and much useful information. Thanks also to my readers Christian MacLean and Norman Shanks for their time and helpful comments.

The Wild Goose Publishing editorial team, Neil Paynter, Sandra Kramer and Jane Darroch Riley, have, as always, shown meticulous attention to detail, dedication to high production values and a com-

mitment and imagination that goes above and beyond the call of
duty. I thank them.

In researching and writing this book, I have discovered the
national treasure that is the Statistical Accounts of Scotland. These,
both the Old Statistical Account of 1791 and the New Statistical
Account of 1845, offer an unparalleled perspective on every part of
Scotland, written at the time. One day, I might disappear into them
and never emerge.

Like so many others, I was inspired and encouraged in my
writing by the late Tom Leonard, poet, writer and critic. I am grateful
to Sonya Leonard and the Tom Leonard Literary Estate for permission to use the poem 'Proem' at the beginning of the book, which is
both an exploration of the question posed by the poem, and the continuation of a conversation.

This book is dedicated to the emerging generation in our family,
and the ones to come.

Kathy Galloway

Introduction

Proem

who are we, trapped in our ways
of dying towards the fact
of only once having been, together

or separate in our own being
but never wholly separate, only a part
of the time we live in, and with others occupy

(Tom Leonard)[1]

On Thursday 24th July, 2014 – a blazingly sunny day in the year of the referendum on Scottish independence and the holding of the Commonwealth Games in Glasgow – I was standing in the garden of a handsome Victorian villa high on a hillside in the village of Kilcreggan on the Firth of Clyde, looking down Loch Long towards the island of Arran.

I was with a dozen others, adults and one little girl. Technically, we were trespassing; we had no authority to be there. We had rung the bell on the front door, but no one was in to ask permission for this garden invasion. We hoped they wouldn't have minded; we intended no ill will. We were there because all of us were descendants of the family who had built the house in 1861 and lived there on and off for more than fifty years. We wanted to see this house which had played an important part in the family's life, and which represented both the highest and the lowest moments in its fortunes.

This visit was part of a family reunion taking place in a (rented) castle in East Ayrshire. One of my brothers, the family historian, had organised this week-long event, and brought together more than twenty people from diverse backgrounds: Scottish, English, Cypriot,

Anglo-Canadian, French Canadian, French, Spanish, Colombian, Japanese. The purpose of the reunion was twofold: to spend time with relatives we saw rarely (and in some instances, had never met) and to explore some of the history of this very dispersed clan; and to celebrate the wedding of one of the Canadian cousins to his Colombian fiancée on the beach at Seamill, further down the Firth of Clyde from Kilcreggan.

Because this family, Campbell by name, had not originated in Kilcreggan, but were actually the descendants of 350 years of Ayrshire farmers, we spent a day in and around the small village of Dalrymple, where generations of them were buried in the church graveyard, and in the larger village of Maybole, five miles away; they farmed between these two places.

But the week also involved much eating and drinking, laughter and talking, sometimes late into the night. We were grateful for the space afforded by the castle to allow us all to meet; none of us has a home which could have accommodated anything near the numbers in this large gathering. Surrounded by ancestral portraits of the great and the good, we enjoyed hearing the history of 'one of Scotland's ancient families'.

This often-used phrase caught my attention. It's usually used in Scotland as a description of the landed aristocracy. But in reality, every single human being alive comes from an ancient family, just by virtue of having been born. What the phrase mostly refers to is those whose continuity of place has lasted for many generations, and whose status has enabled them to have the literacy to record this continuity, the wealth to commission portraiture and sculpture to commemorate it, and in many instances, the power to maintain or enforce it.

There are, of course, ways in which people without these things have marked their familial, communal or tribal history; through oral traditions of story and song, through community or work or spiritual practices, and in many countries, these are still strong. But in Scotland, mobility and migration (forced or otherwise), loss of language, family ties, cultural and labour relationships, have all made the recollection of history and the sharing of memory more difficult.

During that week, therefore, I decided, with great family encouragement, to try to write a history of our own family, drawing on the years of genealogical archaeology undertaken by my brother Callum (in his spare time from being a high school head teacher). This was not a small task. To go back ten generations took us to the late 17th century, when Andrew Campbell, son of John Campbell and Margaret Smith, was born in 1680 in the town of Ayr. This became our starting point. But from that time to this, tracing only direct ancestors, that is, those without whose existence I would never have been born, adds up to a total of 1022 men and women. To write about even a quarter of them would require several volumes. Therefore, this is effectively a history of those we know most about, or who have the most interesting stories, from the late 17th through the 20th centuries in Scotland.

Ours has been a very Scottish family. Out of our thirty direct ancestors back to our great-great-grandparents, all but one, a solitary Irishman, were born, lived and died in Scotland. But members of each of their families left Scotland for many places and for many reasons. We had been the stay-at-home folk; no longer.

In that, we are no different from many Scottish families. We are very ordinary and very typical. Our forebears worked on the land; they were weavers and tradesmen, miners and labourers, ministers and schoolteachers, domestic servants and laundresses. A purely familial history would have been of little interest to those outside our now considerable extended family (and possibly not even to many of them). But I wanted to write something that might speak not just to our children's children, but to others interested in Scottish history viewed from a different perspective.

Our Ayrshire gathering in July 2014 was happening in the midst of a hotly contested, much-commented-upon, referendum on Scottish independence, when people living in Scotland were being asked to vote on whether Scotland should be an independent country, and depart from the union with the rest of the United Kingdom. A huge national debate was taking place, about the politics and economy of Scotland, its governance and the state of its democracy, about poverty and the environment, culture and identity, and what it actually meant to be Scottish. This debate is still going on. I thought that exploring what these things might have looked like to an 18th-century farmer, a 19th-century weaver, a 20th-century coal miner might not only shine a small light on some hidden histories but help me to identify the familial, communal and national forces and influences that have shaped my life, and the lives of others, in Scotland today.

This is, therefore, an eccentric Scottish history. It is not a history of Scotland. It does not represent a view from the centre, or at least from the centre of power. Quite a lot of it is about the things they never taught us in school. Nor is it an academic work (though it has been seriously researched, and draws on much existing historical research). We are often told that it is wrong to read the past through the eyes of the present, or rather, since we can only read from where we are, to pass judgement on the past. But although the facts, as far as we can ascertain, are correct, and the deductions and inferences we have drawn have been a collective family matter, and though any history, however humble, will inevitably be partial and limited, this is a book full of opinions and judgements, for which I take full responsibility. In that regard also, this is an eccentric history.

Note:

1. Proem, by Tom Leonard, from *access to the silence*, etruscan books, 2004. Used by permission of the Tom Leonard Literary Estate

Beginning with the ground, 1680-2020

'A country begins with a ground, a geology. When it loses contact with that, it's no longer a country at all. It's just a supermarket, a Disneyland, or a madhouse.'

(Kenneth White)[1]

The Doon Valley

Andrew Campbell, my six times great-grandfather, was born in Ayr in 1680 to John Campbell and Margaret Smith. He farmed at Piperston in the parish of Dalrymple in the Doon Valley in East Ayrshire for his whole adult life, and he is buried in the graveyard of Dalrymple Parish Church. Subsequently, the descendants of Andrew Campbell and his wife Catherine Hutchison farmed land around Dalrymple and the neighbouring parish of Maybole in an unbroken line for more than three hundred years; one of them was farming in Dalrymple parish in 2014.

Dalrymple is still today a quiet, rural agricultural place. The banks and braes of the River Doon, 'bonnie Doon' as the poet Robert Burns described it (for this was his heartland), still bloom fresh and fair and birds still sing; gentle green hills and small woods cradle a pastoral landscape. You could stand in the churchyard of Dalrymple Church among the old graves looking out over the fields and hedges and imagine you were seeing the same view as Andrew and Catherine would have seen more than three hundred years ago.

It's a wonderfully romantic notion, that of the continuity of the natural landscape. But it's one that needs to be approached with a great deal of caution, because in truth, there is not much that is 'natural' about our natural environment. Our natural landscape in Scotland is also a cultural landscape. Human beings are a small part of the natural history of the earth, but have played a big part in shaping it. Both the beauty of, and the damage to, the natural environment is a product of history and of ecology, of culture as well as of nature.

The human species is a part of the natural order, and in Scotland, our species has acted on our habitat and its resources in order to meet human needs and aspirations for more than six thousand years.

Human impact on nature in Scotland predates the Industrial Revolution, and during Andrew Campbell's lifetime, changes happened which radically altered the landscape of his Ayrshire. For most of this time, the Campbells would have been tenants or subtenants of the Kennedy family, the most powerful aristocratic family in Ayrshire. In the 14th century, the lands and barony of Dalrymple were given to Sir James Kennedy by Robert III, King of Scotland, whose daughter, Princess Mary of Scotland, he was married to. Over the centuries, the Kennedys accumulated land and titles, built castles and abbeys, and feuded mightily among themselves and with other powerful families.

Andrew's many descendants farmed as tenants in several farms within a five-mile radius: Piperston, High and Low Pinmore, Low Milton, Knockjarder, High Skeldon. Land always gives continuity; even so, that one family should have inhabited this small corner of Ayrshire for more than three centuries suggests both a strong attachment to place, and a degree of success in weathering not just the challenges of farming, but also the vagaries of economics, political shifts and the Scottish system of land tenure.

I first encountered feudalism when I was a schoolgirl in Edinburgh in the 1960s, though not, as you might expect, in a history or geography class. The state secondary school that I attended had a school song, which was sung regularly enough that I can still remember every word by heart, more than half a century on. I understand it is still sung today.

We are Vassals of the 'Muir, Vassals of the 'Muir,
In silent vigil at her Shrine, we pledge fealty to the 'Muir.
"Justus! Serve the cause of Right."

"Tenax! Keep the scutcheon bright."
And we proudly bear the Banner, the liege Vassals of the 'Muir.

The 'Muir, the 'Muir, Vassals of the 'Muir,
Rally to the Borestone O ye Vassals of the 'Muir;
To the gate that opens wide,
To the lamp that burns inside,
To the Borestone, to the Borestone,
All ye Vassals of the 'Muir.

How extraordinary this is. A song for Scottish adolescents of the early 21st century, phrased in the terminology of medieval Scotland. I have no idea what our successors make of it, but I remember the glee with which we used to roar out, 'We are barrels of manure, barrels of manure …' Nor do I remember being given any explanation or deconstruction of what it all actually meant, other than that the Borestone was a rallying place for Scottish soldiers gathering for military adventures. Possibly the hapless music teacher who had to teach it to us didn't understand it either.

But I have realised that it's actually a highly educational song. Half the history of Scotland is contained in it, either explicitly or implicitly. The Burgh Muir (from which the school derives its name) is the Scots for 'the town moor', and was a large expanse of ancient forest in the south of the present-day city, given as common land by King David I of Scotland to the then town of Edinburgh in the 12th century. It was cleared of woodland by a decree of James IV in 1508 and used for common grazing land, farmland and building. It was also a traditional location for military training, though one hopes that the students being urged to rally to the Borestone would have more success than those who, in popular belief, mustered there for the Battle of Flodden in 1513, Scotland's worst-ever military defeat.

Other functions of the Burgh Muir were equally grim. It was where victims of the plague, and those who had had contact with them, were quarantined (and often buried) in the 16th and 17th centuries, and it was also a place of public execution at that time, with gypsies and members of the outlawed Clan MacGregor particularly at risk. But these parts of its history are long gone, the Burgh Muir has disappeared under the villas and tenements of south Edinburgh, and the only remnant of the 'common land' is the public park known as Bruntsfield Links, formerly one of the earliest golf courses in Scotland.

The most interesting thing about the song, however, and still with the most contemporary resonances, is the metaphor it uses to encourage its students in their devotion to their school. The terminology is feudal. Feudalism was the most common form of land tenure in Scotland from the 12th century until its abolition in 2004, under the Abolition of Feudal Tenure etc. (Scotland) Act 2000. It was a complex way of structuring a whole society around relationships defined by and deriving from the holding of land in exchange for service, labour and payment of feu (fee) duty. Based on the premise that all land is ultimately owned by the Crown (the monarch, termed the Paramount Superior), charters were granted which defined the rights and privileges being conferred by the Crown, which in the early days of feudalism were predominantly the rights to exercise justice, to receive the profits of justice in terms of fines, and to administer the territory so granted. Charters also specified the obligations required in return, which were to provide military service and feudal payments.

This system then cascaded downwards in what today looks like a long chain of subletting, in which each 'vassal', the person receiving the charter, could in turn grant charters, and become in their turn 'superiors', while still remaining vassals of their own superior. The terms and obligations of each charter remained in force, even if and after the land had been sold. A vassal who had purchased land and now owned it was still bound by the original charter and still owed feu duties to the feudal superior (or actually their heirs, sometimes many centuries later), with whom they had otherwise no connection at all. Since the benefits conferred on the vassal by the charters were now non-existent, the obligations now only flowed upwards. The phrase 'money for old rope' comes to mind.

Feudalism is a complicated system whose definitions and nature continue to be debated widely. But it was the way in which most of Scotland's land was held until very recently, and still has enormous impact today. And perhaps its most important legacy has been a cultural one. The feudal relationship was entered into as a mutual obligation and bond, whereby the vassal made an act of homage, of reverence and submission to the superior, and became quite literally 'his man'. He also swore an oath of fealty; faithfulness was thereby embedded into a relationship which was at its inception a transaction in which land was granted in exchange for military service and loyalty. Much has been made in the past of these as bonds of mutual obligation and protection; they have been promoted as honourable, even sacred, as bonds between free parties.

Though this might be a feasible proposition when pertaining to relationships between powerful members of the medieval aristocracy, it becomes increasingly less convincing the further down the pyramid one goes. The more unequal the participants – in power, in military strength, in wealth and influence, in landholding – the more unfree the vassal, the 'inferior', appears. Certainly, regarding the protection of the weaker by the stronger, it has not demonstrably worked in the interest of the former over the centuries, who have consistently experienced insecurity, indebtedness and poverty at best, and oppression and dispossession at worst. There is little doubt in whose interest it has worked. The marks of the mental submission involved in the need to make a living are still with us to this day.

The period when Andrew Campbell was farming at Piperston was one of considerable change in Scottish agriculture. A decline in the cattle trade, several years of extreme cold weather across Northern Europe, and failed harvests leading to severe famine and depopulation in the 1690s had been catastrophic for Scotland. Tens of thousands of people died of starvation, or took to the roads as beggars in search of food and work. Many thousands more emigrated, either to the American colonies or the West Indies as indentured servants, or to mainland Europe, England or particularly to Ireland. Between 1696-98, around 20,000 migrated to Ulster in the north of Ireland, continuing a process of plantation that had been happening for nearly a century and creating the settler population who came to be known as Ulster Scots. South-west Scotland had long been the main source of migration to Ulster; they are so close geographically that coming and going between the two places was commonplace, and in the 19th century, during the Great Famine in Ireland, the migration was to go in the other direction.

In response to this devastating economic crisis, the Scottish Parliament passed three acts in 1695 which consolidated run rigs (strips of land in communal farming townships) and divided up the common grazing land, creating larger single farms and beginning a process of transformation in Scottish agriculture that was to accelerate during the 18th century. It seems likely that Andrew Campbell and his heirs were winners in this process; there were plenty of losers, not least the cottars, or smallholders, who were gradually displaced or swallowed up by the larger farms. By the 19th century, these peasant farmers, who Burns wrote about in 'The Cottar's Saturday Night' in the 18th century, were gone.

But the most far-reaching consequence of these 'seven ill years', as they became known, was the creation, by an Act of the Scottish Parliament, of an overseas trading company, called The Company of Scotland Trading to Africa and the Indies, which invested a large part of Scotland's capital wealth in a disastrous plan to build a colony on the Isthmus of Panama from where to trade with the East Indies. The multiple failures of the Darien Scheme left the Lowlands of Scotland financially ruined, and bankrupted the Scottish aristocracy. This calamity for Scotland's economy, and for its elites, is seen as one of the key drivers leading to the Treaty of Union of 1706, and the Acts of Union of 1706 and 1707, which brought the United Kingdom of Great Britain into being, against overwhelming opposition from those parts of the Scottish population who found ways of expressing an opinion (they had not been consulted about the union, and had no formal or legal voice in the matter). Opposition was particularly fierce in the Covenanting stronghold of south-west Scotland. Andrew and Catherine Campbell lived through interesting times.

The impact of these turbulent years continued right through the 18th century. In the Old Statistical Account for 1791, when Andrew Campbell's grandson John was farming in Dalrymple, the parish is described as having forty farmers, raising corn, roots, potatoes and cabbages, with enclosures and good roads, and using coal and peat for fuel. The parish also had only seven people on the Poor Roll, and declared that *'no parish in the Presbytery has its poor better supplied'*. Altogether, the minister writing the account felt that *'the people in general are disposed to industry and are economical'*.[2]

But the outlook is not quite so positive in the neighbouring market town of Maybole, five miles away, also a place of significance for the Campbell family. Here there is a lot of wool manufacturing, mostly blanket-making, employing three hundred people. But, unlike in Dalrymple, there are considerable numbers of the poor, *'partly from the great number of the inhabitants [around 800], and partly from the great influx of vagrants from Ireland. It may be said that in this parish, the poor maintain the poor. Few of the principal heritors [local landholders] reside in the parish, and nothing is given by them in the way of donation to the poor, who are maintained wholly by the collections made at the church door, upon Sunday. For that reason, though the contributions are very liberal, considering the small fortunes of the persons by whom they are given, the poor of this parish do not receive even one half of what they would require.'*[3] The writer, the Rev. Dr James Wright, does, however, note the excellence of Maybole's water supply, which, along with its dry situation and southerly exposure, accounts for the great health and longevity of its inhabitants, including several centenarians.

By the middle of the 19th century, when my great-great-grandfather John Campbell was the tenant of the Marquis of Ailsa at Knockjarder Farm, Dalrymple was a settled and thriving village, with wheat, oats and dairy being the main agricultural produce. It had two schools, a Friendly Society, a Musical Society, a Burns Club and a curling club. The Savings Bank in Maybole received more contributions from the parish of Dalrymple than from any of the other surrounding parishes; a sign of its prosperity, perhaps. The local schoolmaster described the peaceful inhabitants as characterised by decency, sobriety and orderly conduct. All but a few Dissenters adhered to the Establishment (the Church of Scotland).

The Ayrshire Campbells were the ancestors of my paternal grandmother, Marion Campbell. For the best part of two hundred years, they were born, lived and died in Dalrymple. They married people from Dalrymple, or nearby parts of Ayrshire. But in 1872, Henry Campbell married Margaret McLellan, a young woman from a Paisley family, and eventually moved with her to the villa in Kilcreggan, where my grandmother was born.

The Merchant City and the public square

The family of my paternal grandfather, Robert Orr, were deeply rooted in the city of Glasgow. When the Orr ancestors appear in the records in 1704, Glasgow had already seen gradual change from its centuries of being a small fishing and farming village on the River Clyde, gathered round a religious and monastic settlement, its 12th-century cathedral (the oldest building in the city) and then its medieval university, one of the oldest in Europe, founded in 1451. It had modest trade, mostly in fish, to the Low Countries and the Baltic region.

Glasgow's fortunes took a great leap forward in the 17th century.

The Trades House and the Merchants House, both established in 1605, and the city becoming a Royal Burgh in 1611, emphasised the growing importance of trade and manufacture to the city's economy. But the real boost to its wealth was the expansion of Atlantic trade, in sugar and tobacco, then cotton and linen. All of these were commodities of, and enabled by, the triangular Atlantic slave trade.

In 1704, the population of Glasgow was still only around 12,000. But unparalleled change was on its way. The Acts of Union of 1707 meant that Scotland now had access to the huge markets of the ever-expanding British Empire. The creation of a deep-water port at Port Glasgow, further down the Clyde, with the deepest and most sheltered coastal waters in Britain, meant a greatly enlarged transatlantic trading capacity and made Glasgow a hub for international trade, and an increasingly important commercial city. The major beneficiaries of this activity were the merchants and slave traders, whose enormous fortunes led them to become known as the Tobacco Lords. These newly and fabulously rich merchants then invested their wealth into their homes, offices and churches, raising mansions in what is now known as the Merchant City, and beginning to create the built environment of modern Glasgow. They marked their involvement in, and indeed their dependence on, the slave trade and plantation slavery by giving their own names, and the names of the places their wealth derived from, to the street names of central Glasgow, which still bear these names. Meanwhile, and perhaps somewhat peripherally to the lives of ordinary Glaswegians, the Scottish Enlightenment was coming into full flower in the lecture rooms and clubs around Glasgow University.

By the time that my great-great-great-grandfather, John Orr, married Jean McNair in Paisley in 1797, the city's population had increased sixfold, to around 70,000 inhabitants. But the 19th century hugely accelerated the pace and nature of growth and change. John Orr was a farmer from Renfrew, a few miles west of Glasgow where the River Cart joins the Clyde. Rapid industrialisation was sweeping away the surrounding farmlands; the many thousands of small artisan trades still in existence during the 18th century were supplanted or rendered redundant. Canals were opened, giving access to coal and iron-ore mines inland from Glasgow to deep-water ports on the Clyde. Shipbuilding became a major industry along the river; engineering, machine-making, chemicals, textiles, garment-making, printing and publishing – if it could be made, it was made in Glasgow. And the financial and legal services required for such an expansion enabled the rise of a new professional and trading middle class.

The city expanded outwards and upwards in an attempt to cope with a huge population increase. Migration from the rural south-west counties of Scotland, land workers forced to move by the disappearance of their livelihoods during the Lowland agricultural clearances, and from the Highlands during their clearances, was significantly increased by migration from Ireland, particularly during the years of the Great Famine. By 1831, the city's population had outstripped that of Edinburgh, the capital of Scotland, and was now over 200,000. But even if there were jobs – in factories, yards and ironworks – there were not enough places for them to live. In 1831, the population density per square kilometre was a truly horrifying 23,000.

Dozens of villages on the banks of the Clyde and its tributaries, the Kelvin to the north and the Cart to the south, were swallowed up in this urban expansion. But most of all, the city built: tens of thousands of the tenement buildings which became characteristic of Glasgow, and which is still its commonest type of dwelling. Built from red or honey sandstone quarried from the south-west of Scotland, their uniform external design concealed great internal variation – from the 'single end' (in which living, sleeping and cooking areas were all contained within one room), and the 'room and kitchen' (as it sounds, often with a bed recess in the kitchen), to grand six- or seven-roomed apartments with bay windows, stained-glass panels in the doors and intricate cornicing. Very few of the tenements had internal plumbing or sanitation, instead, people made do with a shared lavatory in the back court, or if they were better-off, on the stair landing, with a hand pump in the street for water. Broadly speaking, the burgeoning middle classes lived in tenements to the west of the city centre, while the working poor were crammed into much smaller flats in the East End. As the rich got richer, and the middle classes flourished, the poor became poorer to an appalling degree.

But Glasgow could not keep pace with the insatiable demand for labour in its building programme. The city centre and East End tenements became hopelessly overcrowded and unhealthy, a breeding ground for diseases such as cholera, typhoid and tuberculosis. The website of the Glasgow Britannia Panopticon (the world's oldest surviving music hall) offers a vivid description of the city in the middle of the 19th century:

'Thousands of workers had flocked to the city to work in the mills, factories, foundries, shipyards and collieries. They lived in the worst conditions imaginable; single ends housed one third of the population, lodging houses where they crammed eight to a bed were available for those who couldn't afford a single end and if you couldn't afford a sliver of bed space then the penny line was a slightly better option than the poorhouses and workhouses. (A Penny Line was a washing line – sometimes also referred to as the penny lean – which would hold the sleeper up by the oxters [armpits] until the line was untied the following morning.)

'The social and working conditions of the workers of this industrial empire were not so much intangible as unimaginable to us today; men, women and children toiled in the most atrocious and dangerous conditions, the stench of the sewers, the thick smoke that belched from the factories and mills and made the air thick

and foul to breathe, the lack of indoor and outdoor plumbing etc.
would be insufferable to our modern and delicate dispositions –
only the strongest survived.'[4]

Numerous of my family lived in 19th-century Glasgow tenements,
in both the western parts of the city, and in the less salubrious parts
of the city centre and the south side. I have myself lived in four tenement flats: in the East End, in Govan and in the West End. In spite
of all the developments that came afterwards – the slum clearance
and rebuilding that took place in the late 19th century, the major
programme of tenement demolition of the 1960s and '70s, and their
replacement by high-rise blocks (many of them also now demolished) – it is the tenements of Glasgow which give it its distinctive
architectural identity as a Victorian city.

This was an era when many of the city's great civic building and
engineering projects took place, and nowhere is this more evident
than in the city's heart, George Square. Over its more than two centuries of existence, this public square has manifested the realms of
commerce, media, politics, education, science and society. Nor has
this been a purely local or even national manifestation. Indeed, the
very architecture of the square tells its own story:

- *its Enlightenment Georgian layout and buildings set it within the*
  context of a European philosophical movement;

- *its ship on the globe on top of the Chamber of Commerce a*
  reminder that globalisation is not a new phenomenon in a mer-
  cantile city;

- *the central column of the Square, revealing the angst of the*
  Tobacco Lords, who substituted Walter Scott in place of George
  III, a kind of code which hid the fact that their wealth and gentility
  was firmly founded on the produce of slavery;

- *the magnificent City Chambers with its marble floors and Glasgow Boys murals, built by Victorian municipal socialism, a contradiction in an industrial city which became 'the second city of the Empire', taking its very unequally-shared prosperity from an imperial capitalism, built by the sweat of some of the most appallingly housed and paid workers in the world.*

The built environment of George Square speaks of power, wealth and influence, then and now: the grand hotels and office buildings, the pub and restaurant chains, the accountancy firms and multinationals. But the public *space* of the square – that's a different story. It's the space occupied by the disenfranchised and the dispossessed, the marginalised and the unnumbered. The story of the public square, certainly in Glasgow and I suspect in many, many places, is the story of the conflict between the powerful and the powerless. George Square is a cogent reminder that its citizens live in the built environment of white supremacy. It represents a democratic deficit, because it was built before universal suffrage in Britain, and because it was built at the expense of the majority of the population; the majority in Glasgow but also the majority in the tobacco plantations of Louisiana and Jamaica, the majority in the jute and cotton mills of India, the majority in the copper mines of Zambia and the gold mines of South Africa. This is particularly evident in the statues around the square.

They are all of white, Protestant men, apart from Queen Victoria, and the only poor person Glasgow has honoured is Robert Burns. At least half of them owe their exalted positions to slavery. They are really a memorial to the British Empire, which gave most of them their wealth and power, and to a relationship with Ireland in which Scotland has continually sought to assert its superiority. Glasgow has a sorry history of sectarianism, which is intimately tied up with the history of Ireland. Throughout the 19th century and well into the 20th century, there was significant migration from Catholic Ireland into the West of Scotland, overwhelmingly as the result of poverty, particularly the potato famines. At around the same time, the Clearances drove dispossessed Presbyterian Highland and Lowland Scots to the city of Glasgow, where they all became the labour that kept the engines of 'the workshop of the world' turning. They lived in the most appalling conditions of squalor, overcrowding and disease, racked by cholera and extreme poverty. In the context of competition for survival and scarce resources, what was essentially an economic problem became entangled with issues of religion, culture and identity. People who really had far more in common than what divided them entered a kind of war of attrition, played out on football fields, in factories and in neighbourhoods.

The square has often been the scene of public meetings, political gatherings, riots, protests, celebrations, ceremonies, parades and concerts. Perhaps the most famous was the Black Friday 1919 rally, when campaigners for improved working conditions (particularly protesting a 56-hour working week in many of the city's factories) held an enormous demonstration, with at least 90,000 protesters filling the square and the surrounding streets. The meeting descended into violence between the protesters and the police, with the Riot Act being read. The city's radical reputation, and the raising of the red flag by some present, made the Coalition government fear a Bolshevik revolution was afoot. The government responded by deploying fully-armed troops and tanks into the square and the city's streets. George Square is still the place where Glaswegians go to protest, which they do often.

On one edge of George Square, there is a small stone set into the ground. It's a memorial stone laid by Glasgow members of ATD Fourth World, a human rights movement of people living in poverty started by a French priest, Father Joseph Wresinski. It honours the countless citizens of Glasgow over many centuries who died of poverty. They had to fight to get permission to lay it. It's not grand, it's not artistic, and the stone-carving is worn. Most people don't notice it. But it's there. It's a reminder of the people who really made Glasgow.

There have been members of my family living in Glasgow continuously for over three hundred years. Today, to the best of my knowledge, I am the last one still here. But I will never leave.

An austere landscape

The family of my maternal grandfather, Clement Johnston, belonged to another part of Scotland, the east central counties of Stirling and West Lothian. Walter Johnston, my five times great-grandfather, married Elizabeth Ramsay in 1731 in the medieval village of Bathgate, West Lothian. Bathgate is just a couple of miles from a Neolithic burial site at Cairnpapple Hill, and the area has signs of human habitation since about 3500 BC. Walter and Elizabeth's son John also lived in Bathgate, a small, rural, agricultural community then (and for a century to come), worked as a miller, and married Margaret Aitken from the nearby village of Kirknewton.

It was their son, another John, who took a new direction which radically altered the whole trajectory of my family ever since. He moved nine miles north to Polmont, above the carse lands of the Forth Valley, mostly agricultural land reclaimed from peat bog. Down this coastal estuary was easy access to the port of Grangemouth, and coal reserves were beginning to be mined on an increasingly large scale. We don't know whether John worked his way up from the coalface at the Redding Collieries, but by the 1830s, he was the colliery manager. For 150 years, generation after generation of my family were coal miners, then shale miners, then coal miners again, or worked in ancillary or service trades in the mining industry. Seventeen direct ancestors worked in and around the pits in these years, and many more brothers, cousins, uncles.

Gradually they moved south and east, a few miles at a time, every few years, as seams closed out and were opened up elsewhere; from Polmont to Muiravonside, from Slamannan to Woodmuir, to Loganlea and Addiewell, West Calder and Mossend, and finally to

Stoneyburn, where in 1913, Clement Johnston, my maternal grand-father, married Sarah Thomson.

In a country of beautiful landscapes, West Lothian is mostly low-lying and rural, either farmland or moorland. It's dotted with pit bings (raised heaps of mining residue) and industrial and commercial buildings, many of them disused. It's a county of dozens of small villages, many of them former mining villages, and a few larger towns. The mining villages today have often been extensively rebuilt, and maybe twenty of these former settlements have disappeared altogether – the lost villages of West Lothian.

In the 19th century, much of the housing, and all of it in the lost villages, was built by the coal and shale companies to house their workers, very close to the mines so that, without public or private transport, the miners could walk to work. The companies built as cheaply as they could: without building regulations, standards or inspections, without water supply, adequate drainage or sewage systems, and without roads or street lighting. Though there were exceptions, the vast majority of miners lived in one-storey, brick-built row housing in squalid and sometimes dangerous conditions. Since it was tied accommodation, miners were reluctant to complain about the conditions in case they lost their jobs. As it was, when the pits were worked-out and closed, the villages were demolished, or fell into such dilapidation that they were eventually declared unfit for human habitation. The miners' rows at Woodmuir, where my grand-mother Sarah was born in 1893, was to become one of the lost villages.

In the second half of the 19th century, and well into the 20th, one could well describe West Lothian as an austere landscape. The word 'austerity', which has come back into currency in the last decade or so, comes from the Latin root for *dry, harsh or stern*. My dictionaries offer a number of alternative meanings for austere. They include:

- *Harsh, stern, forbidding (referring to manners or moral conditions)*

- *Severely simple (referring to mode of life)*
- *Severe, sparing, chaste (referring to literary style).*

They also include:

- *Frugal, lean*
- *Rigorous, exacting, searching, plain*
- *Self-disciplined or ascetic*
- *Reduced availability of luxuries and consumer goods.*

I have to confess that I do not find all of these meanings entirely unappealing. I am, after all, a Scottish Presbyterian from a country of wild terrain and harsh weather, for whom, in some interpretations, the word 'austere' might have been coined. For sure, the landscapes that speak strongest to my heart are those which many find stern or forbidding – the treeless hills of the Southern Uplands, the bogs and moors of the Ross of Mull, the hard and empty grandeur of the Scottish north-west, the windswept, storm-tossed islands of Shetland. These are austere landscapes, yet they are also beautiful. But for many, they would be defined by what they lack – lushness, productivity, utility, shelter, 'civilisation'.

19th-century West Lothian did not lack productivity, and its products of coal and shale oil were intensely useful in both driving the industrialisation of Britain, and turning the wheels of the British Empire. But apart from the privileged few, lushness would not be an apt description for the lives of most of its people, whose shelter was sadly lacking in amenity. Civilisation? A good question. Much of the natural environment was scarred by excavation, polluted and despoiled, rendered harsh, stern and forbidding.

When the UK prime minister, David Cameron, announced '*a new age of austerity*' in 2009, what he really meant was massive and sustained cuts in public spending, which was the policy programme duly carried out in the next seven years of Conservative government. This new age of austerity was also framed as lack; in this context as a lack of money, shown by high levels of personal and public debt, and by unsustainable budget deficits. The solution to the problem of this apparent lack of money, this deficiency, was framed as cuts, the reduction of public services and welfare payments. People would have to make do with less, they would have to be more frugal, and they would need to live a more severely simple lifestyle. If they were reluctant or unable to do this voluntarily, there would be sanctions; they might lose their social security payments; they might lose their homes. The public services which have enabled the very young, the very old, the sick and disabled, the unemployed, struggling families, to access at least a few of the freedoms that many of us take for granted – mobility, support in times of crisis, recourse to the justice and legal systems, affordable housing – would all be reduced, and in some instances stripped away altogether.

This is indeed what happened, and with some quite unexpected consequences – a global pandemic has cruelly exposed the impact of austerity on the NHS and the greatly increased social and economic inequality, which has been another consequence, has shown up in increased mortality rates in the poorest and most vulnerable communities. The 21st-century age of austerity has proved to be pretty much like the 19th century, West Lothian variety: austerity for the many, huge profit for the few.

In his splendid essay titled simply 'Austerity', the historian Tony Judt revisited another Age of Austerity – the immediate post-war years in 20th-century Britain. Differentiating between austerity and poverty, he remembered that rationing and subsidies meant that the bare necessities of life were accessible to all, with free milk and orange juice for the children. He suggests that austerity in post-war Britain was not just an economic condition, but that it aspired to be a public ethos, exemplified in its moral seriousness by Clement Attlee, the greatest reformer in modern British history. He claims that the opposite of austerity is not prosperity but *luxe et volupté*, luxury and pleasure.[5] It was the 20th-century Age of Austerity, with its post-war reforms and public ethos, which finally lifted my own West Lothian Johnston family out of the poverty, disease and premature death which had stalked them for 150 years.

Away to the west

Away to the west, the family of my maternal grandmother, Sarah Thomson, was beginning to wend its way towards Stoneyburn, West Lothian, where Sarah met Clement Johnston. But the Thomson journey was both more complicated and more diverse than that of the Johnstons. They were the poorest family over generations, and because of that, they moved more frequently, moved further and turned their hands to many more occupations.

Like the Campbells, they came from Ayrshire, and worked on the land. But unlike the Campbells, they were not settled and secure tenant farmers, but landless labourers, moving their large families from farm to farm, wherever they could get work. So my great-great-great-grandfather, Alexander Thomson, born in 1807 in Cumnock, the son of John Thomson, a cotton weaver, married Mary Clark, born in 1807 in Straiton, who came from a long line of Ayrshire farmers, whose roots can be traced back to the early 17th century. Alexander and Mary had eleven children, eight daughters and three sons. They are recorded as living at several farms, where Alexander was a general labourer: Burnside, Braehead and the picturesquely named Dunnymuck, where my great-great-grandfather John Thomson was born in 1832.

John was a farm servant at Turnberry Lodge, and he died before he was thirty, though not before marrying Elizabeth Aitken and having five children with her. The family had moved first to Ayr, then to Cadder and Milton in the north of Glasgow, where John died. The second of these children, Thomas Thomson, worked variously as a flour miller, a railway carter, and a labourer stoking coke ovens until, after thirty years in Glasgow, he moved east to the pit at

Woodmuir in West Lothian.

Thomas had married Sarah Wallis Smith Morrin, a chemical worker in Glasgow, in 1873. Sarah's family origins lie the furthest to the west of all my ancestors. Her father, Maurice Morrin, was an immigrant from Ireland, who had mostly worked as a coachman/domestic servant and an omnibus driver in Cardross and Glasgow, but he too eventually moved east, to work as a pithead labourer and eventually lodging-house keeper in Whitburn, just four miles from Stoneyburn. This was really a family move; Sarah's two brothers had also moved to work at Woodmuir Colliery. Sarah's mother, Marrion Gilchrist, came from a family of weavers and crofters on the island of Islay, where her father had been the local schoolmaster. These two Gaels, Maurice and Marrion, are my only ancestors who did not originate in the Scottish Lowlands. But their journeys are part of the movement east whereby Sarah Wallis Smith Morrin Thomson met and married Clement Johnston, shale and coal miner, in Stoneyburn.

The North Clyde Line

Over nearly 350 years, almost my entire family has lived between the Highland Boundary Fault and the Southern Uplands Fault, or, more poetically, between the Antonine Wall and a bit to the north of Hadrian's Wall, in the Lowlands of Scotland. Until well into the 19th century, they lived in their own small areas of the Lowlands – East and South Ayrshire, Renfrewshire and Glasgow and West Lothian for generation after generation, moving no more than a few miles for work or marriage, however often they did move. The great change in the radius of their mobility came from about the 1840s onward, with the introduction of the railways. Not only could coal and iron and timber and livestock be carried to the factories and the ports of the rapidly industrialising Lowlands, so could the people. All of Scotland's present-day network of railways has been formed by the merging and consolidation of numerous minor, privately-owned lines in the 20th century onwards.

What is today the Inverclyde Line carried Maurice Morrin from Ireland onward into Scotland from the port of Greenock. It took Adam McLellan from Paisley to Gourock to catch the ferry to Kilcreggan, where he built his villa, Albert Park. It took the vintner George Lyall from his Paisley properties into Glasgow Central to visit his Glasgow wine cellar.

The South Western Line took John Fleming from his home in Girvan into Glasgow to pursue his horticultural training at the Botanic Gardens. It took Elizabeth Aitken Thomson and her five children into Glasgow from Maybole, then Elizabeth home to Ayrshire again thirty years later to die in Maybole, and Henry Campbell from Maybole to Paisley to marry Margaret McLellan. It took Catherine Lyall with her parents from Paisley to West Kilbride for a seaside holiday.

But my favourite line is what is today known as the North Clyde Line. I don't drive, and have travelled a great deal in Scotland for business, family and pleasure, very often on this line. I think of it as my family line. It starts in Helensburgh, where my grandmother, May Campbell Orr, newly widowed, retired to a little house in 1950, and where we often spent holidays with cousins, swimming in the freezing outdoor pool, playing on the beach, visiting the public library. The next stop is Craigendoran, where May and her Campbell siblings got off the ferry from Kilcreggan as children in the 1890s to attend school in Helensburgh. Then Cardross, where John Fleming the gardener eventually became Head Gardener at Kilmahew Castle, and where Maurice Morrin was the coachman to another large house. At Dalreoch, where Robert Orr, May's husband, was the parish minister, the four Orr sons got the train to Glasgow, to go to university, to work, and eventually to war.

The train travels along the River Clyde, and then through the outer suburbs of Glasgow, stopping off at Anniesland, where

Netherton, home of James Orr senior and Agnes Hamilton, was swallowed up by Glasgow; then from Hyndland into the leafy streets of the West End, where the sisters May, Kit and Peggy Campbell all spent their last years in tenement flats within walking distance of each other. Charing Cross is close to the large flat to which Margaret McLellan Campbell decamped each year for decades so that she could let out the Kilcreggan villa.

The line continues on through the city centre, stopping at Bellgrove station in the East End to pick up the Thomson men en route to Woodmuir Colliery from the Springburn interchange. Then out of the city, through the post-industrial and commuter towns of North Lanarkshire, and the farming lands that lead into West Lothian. There used to be a railway station at Bents, which served Stoneyburn, but it's long closed, so the Thomson men and the Morrin men, now related by marriage, would today have got off the train at Armadale, or Bathgate. And there would be Johnstons too, coming and going around the pits of West Lothian. And finally, in 1934, Sarah Johnston, now widowed, would get on with her seven children (five of them under ten years old) and get off at Haymarket, where they lived for a few years before getting a flat in the new council scheme of West Pilton, where our mother Janet Johnston met our father Jack Orr.

All of these people – this is their country; these are their stories.

Notes:

1. Kenneth White, from 'The Re-mapping of Scotland' in *The Wanderer and His Charts: Essays on Cultural Renewal*, Polygon, 2004. Reproduced with permission of the Licensor through PLSclear

2. From the Statistical Account of Scotland 1791:
   https://stataccscot.edina.ac.uk/static/statacc/dist/home

3. ibid. 2

4.   From 'Britannia Panopticon Music Hall – Life in Old Ghost', by Judith
     Bowers, on the Britannia Panopticon website:
     www.britanniapanopticon.org/history.
     Originally from *Glasgow's Lost Theatre: The Story of the Britannia Music
     Hall*, Judith Bowers, Birlinn, 2014. Used by permission of Judith Bowers

5.   'Austerity' in *The Memory Chalet*, Tony Judt, William Heinemann, 2010

About the fathers, 1800-1900

Like many people in Scotland, where only one in a hundred still work in agriculture, my closest, hands-on connection with the land is as a gardener, and it's urban. I garden what is essentially a Glasgow back court, complete with midden shed, in an overambitious and haphazard fashion. In an area 15x10 metres, I maintain a woodland patch with five trees, a rockery, a gravel garden, herbaceous and perennial borders, and grow vegetables, soft fruit and herbs with varying degrees of success. Effectively I have realised that I am trying to make a large garden in a small space, I have no formal knowledge of gardening at all, and the whole thing is very labour-intensive. But it has been created out of what was formerly waste ground full of builders' rubble, has been a major point of contact and shared enthusiasm with the other inhabitants of the building, and brings me great pleasure, a fair degree of exercise and the chance to be often outside in the middle of a city.

Perhaps the desire to make a large garden is part of what shaped the working life of **John Fleming**. Born in 1818 in Girvan in Ayrshire, he moved to Glasgow in 1841 to train as a gardener in Glasgow Botanic Gardens in their new site at the end of the street where his great-great-granddaughter now lives. Subsequently, he worked in a series of grand houses: at Culcreuch in Fintry, then at Bloomhill in Cardross, about 20 miles north-west of Glasgow on the north shore of the River Clyde in the county of Argyll. Bloomhill was owned by James Burns, who had bought it from the family of Alexander Ferrier, one of the most notorious Scottish slave owners, on his death. James Burns also owned the Kilmahew Estate, and John Fleming then worked at Kilmahew House.

The Kilmahew Estate has an interesting history. Its name is ancient, from the Gaelic word '*cille*' referring to a settlement of monks and the name *Mahew*, a 6th-century Celtic missionary monk, and there is an early Christian chapel here, with evidence of an earlier pagan sanctuary. By the late 13th century, the land was in the hands of the powerful Napier clan, whose ruined castle sits in

Kilmahew Glen. By the early 19th century, the estate had been sold to pay for the expensive tastes and the gambling debts of the last Napier laird, and now belonged to the Burns family, wealthy industrialists who made a fortune in shipping. James Burns built a handsome baronial mansion, Kilmahew House, and redesigned the landscape around it, creating a Victorian garden in a romantic style, with waterfalls and bridges, a walled garden and formal terracing, and a rhododendron tunnel.

In 1948, the estate was bought by the Roman Catholic Archdiocese of Glasgow and became a seminary for the training of priests. A new complex of modernist buildings embraced the Victorian mansion, in a radical design by Glasgow architectural firm Gillespie, Kidd & Coia that was seen as one of Britain's greatest architectural commissions of the 20th century. But St Peter's College, as it was now known, was only in use for fourteen years; declining numbers were entering the priesthood, and a design and materials unsuited to the damp West of Scotland climate rendered the building unfit for alternative use. It closed in 1980, and rapidly fell into disrepair and decay. The old mansion house, twice set on fire, was pulled down for safety reasons in 1995, and only the foundations remain today. Years of neglect and abandonment have placed this great architectural landmark of modernism on a list of the world's one hundred most endangered buildings; ambitious plans by Scottish arts charity NVA to buy the whole site and reinvent it as an Invisible College have collapsed because of funding shortages.

But it was in the Victorian Kilmahew that John Fleming began work as a gardener, rising to become a master gardener and eventually Head Gardener. He also wrote several books on horticulture, drawing on his extensive knowledge of the local landscape and his hands-on kitchen garden experience growing flowers, fruit and vegetables for the house: *The Open Flower Garden; Fruit: A treatise on the vine, pine-apple, peach, plum, nectarine &c; Kitchen, Fruit and Flower Manual* and the one that sits on my own bookshelf, *Botanical*

Guide to the Wild Flowers in the West of Scotland. In a lengthy and rather remarkable introduction to this last, which includes a brief biography of his hero, Carl Linnaeus, before going on to a detailed description of Linnaean classification, John Fleming writes:

> 'The investigation of the phenomena of the material universe, by bringing within the scope of human thought and feeling the grand, the good and the beautiful, enlarges and ennobles the mind, improves and elevates the heart, cultivates and refines the taste, and thus proves a source of pure and rational gratification. Accordingly, the wise and good of all times have found congenial employment in tracing the footsteps of the Creator in the wise adaptations, the benevolent designs, and the exquisitely delicate touches of beauty everywhere discernible in the works of His hands. And surely the accumulated stores of scientific knowledge are now the common inheritance of mankind. The arts of life springing therefrom, which have contributed so largely to the commerce, the happiness and embellishment of society have amply rewarded the research and thought expended in the inquiry. What has thus been won for science and the progressive improvement and happiness of mankind must be enjoyed, perpetuated and increased by the same means ... the study of Botany is important as an intellectual exercise. The mastery of its numerous details cannot fail to invigorate, while it interests the mind ... every well-regulated mind feels an interest in Botany.'[1]

Here, only twenty years after Charles Darwin published *The Origin of the Species*, in the characteristic overblown style of the time, the Victorian myth of progress meets 'the light of the mind'.

In 2004, Edwin Morgan, the Scots Makar (Poet Laureate), wrote a poem, 'Open the Doors!', for the inauguration of the new Scottish Parliament.

Open the doors! Light of the day, shine in; light of the mind,
shine out!
We have a building which is more than a building.
There is a commerce between inner and outer,
between brightness and shadow,
between the world and those who think about the world. [2]

And then ...

Come down the Mile, into the heart of the city, past the kirk
of St Giles and the closes and wynds of the noted ghosts of
history who drank their claret and fell down the steep
tenements stairs into the arms of link-boys but who wrote
and talked the starry Enlightenment of their days — [3]

I remember a friend, an Oxford academic, remarking that England had never really had an Enlightenment and that that explained a lot! Be that as it may, historians tell us that one of the main factors which brought about the Enlightenment in Europe in the 18th century, which saw the value of freedom of conscience, religious tolerance and the move towards democracy, was that Europe was simply exhausted, nauseated to the point of death by a century of religious wars and the destruction of habitats, and something like common sense finally prevailed. In the 17th century, especially during the Thirty Years War, interminable religious conflicts had raged back and forth across Europe, rendering much of it a blackened charnel house in which millions, not just soldiers, were butchered, starved, or frozen to death, or perished in one of the periodic outbreaks of the Black Death and thousands of women were burned as witches. The value and importance of simply being human, of the right to life, broke through the culture of death and the competing ideologies.

The leading thinkers and scholars of the Scottish Enlightenment, philosophers and scientists, asserted the fundamental importance of human reason combined with a rejection of any authority which could not be justified by reason and observation. They held to an optimistic belief in the ability of human beings to effect changes for the better in society and nature. This methodology, known as empiricism, held the view that knowledge is gained primarily through sensory experience and observation, in which evidence, tested against observation of the natural world, is vital. Its principles were those of equality, progress and practical outcomes in daily life, benefiting society as a whole. Empiricism is a basis of scientific methodology.

Many claims have been made for the importance of the Scottish Enlightenment, not least that through its importance and impact, the Scots invented the modern world. If this is the case, is that a good thing? Perhaps that depends on where one lives in the modern world. Certainly, one of the major areas of contention for the Scottish Enlightenment, and what came after, was the relationship between science and religion, expressed more acutely in the 19th century in Darwinian debates, still very much alive today. This contention was sometimes a battleground with many casualties, sometimes a dialogue, sometimes so profoundly oppositional that it has completely severed parts of the Christian church from an appreciation, or even an understanding of, science, and from other parts of the church. But for many, these two, science and religion, were not oppositional at all, as they seem not to have been for John Fleming.

***

Meanwhile, back in the late 19th century, while my paternal great-great-grandfather was making gardens and exploring the light of the mind in writing books, my maternal great-great-grandfather, **James Lamond**, was mining shale in West Lothian. The Scottish shale oil industry has an interesting and important history. Its Bathgate works, established in 1851, was perhaps the first site in the world where mineral oils were processed on an industrial scale. Initially intended to produce lubricating oil, it was soon appreciated that a market existed also for lighter oils that could be burned in lamps.

The promise of clean affordable domestic lighting brought an immediate demand for the new lamp oil, and immense public interest. From this blossomed an extensive oil industry that competed successfully against cheaper imported petroleum for many years, and continued in operation until 1962. Such fierce competition bred innovation, progress, and a body of Scots know-how that contributed much towards the development of the oil industry throughout the world.

A Mr David Bremner wrote in 1869 about James Young, the chemist and entrepreneur who developed shale mining in Addiewell, a West Lothian village where another great-great-grandfather, **Clement Johnston**, lived and worked as a joiner:

> *'It has been rarely that an inventor has lived to see such a splendid outcome of his ideas, or to be a partaker, as Mr Young has been, of the wealth created by his discoveries. To anyone who takes an intelligent interest in the manufacturing industries of the world, there could be few things more enjoyable than to walk over the great chemical manufactory at Addiewell in company with Mr Young, and hear him quietly relate, in answer to your queries, how he devoted himself to reveal some of the mysteries of nature, and convert to the use of mankind what were apparently the meanest among the contents of her storehouse.'*[4]

Mr Bremner also noted that *'the houses provided for the workpeople are commodious and comfortable, and they are let at very moderate rents'*.[5] It all sounds very enlightened. However, a report on housing conditions in the Scottish shale fields in 1914 paints a somewhat different picture of housing conditions in Addiewell:

> *'In the village, there are some 360 houses built of brick, in rows and tenements. There are some 70 single-apartment houses, and about 290 two-apartment houses. No wash-houses are provided for any of the tenants, and 90 have no coal-cellars.*

*'The size of single apartments is 14 feet 10 inches by 12 feet;
height 8 feet 10 inches. In two-apartment houses the kitchen
measures 13 ft. by 11 ft., and the room 9.5 ft. by 11 ft.; height 8
ft. 7 inches in some houses, in others the height measures 9 feet 3
inches. A number of houses have gardens.*

*'For about 300 houses there are only twelve privies of a most objec-
tionable character. Ash-pits are provided, but they are built from
about 15 to 20 yards from the houses, and as can readily be imagined, they are a positive pestilence in the summer time, and at all
times a danger to the health of the community. Clothes poles are
studded here and there in the back courts. Water is procured from
some seventeen stand-pipes, and the sewage flows down by open
channels. The sanitary conditions generally existing are bad in the
extreme. The rental is 2/4 per week for double- and 1/6. per week
for single-apartment houses, inclusive of local and county rates.
The houses are occupied principally by the oil workers.*

*'An Institute with library and reading room is provided, also room
for games, for which the workers are charged 1d. per week.*

*'The houses are owned by Messrs Young's Oil Company. In
Addiewell district there are some 650 houses, with a population
of 2100 persons.'*[6]

But it wasn't just shale that was being extracted in West Lothian.
For more than a hundred years, my mother's family were coal miners
in the pits which dotted the county, living in the small villages of
the Central Belt. I trace their gradual movement eastward on the
map of Scotland, from Kirkintilloch and Slamannan, from Polmont
and Bathgate, eventually settling in the cluster a few miles square
which includes West Calder, Addiewell, Fauldhouse, Loganlea,
Woodmuir, Whitburn and Stoneyburn, where my mother was born
in 1931.

The Scottish Mining Website carries dozens of descriptions of miners' housing, in reports made in 1875, 1910, 1918, and all show the same picture: the vast majority lived in accommodation which was damp, squalid, lacking in basic services and clean water, and completely inadequate for families and their health. This is a report on housing in Mossend, West Calder, where James Lamond lived with his wife and seven children:

> 'These rows also belong to Young's Mineral Oil Company. There are 140 double-apartment houses. The water is supplied by four stand-pipes. The rental is 2s. 3d. per week, inclusive of rates. There are no coal-collars, wash-houses, or sculleries. Dry privies exist, but they are practically public nuisances. The refuse is removed weekly by the Oil Company. The sewage is disposed of by open channel. There is a contrast in black and white about these houses – the gables are blackened with tar, while the fronts and backs of the houses are whitewashed.

> 'In West Calder district there are approximately some 1010 houses occupied by 4220 persons.

> 'The housing conditions in West Calder district are very unsatisfactory. It is a mild expression to say they are disgraceful, and the wonder is that the public authorities tolerate such conditions. Owing to recent developments of mining, there is a great scarcity of houses, and the County Council ought to build to meet requirements. The Council have been approached, but little encouragement has been held out that they will build houses to meet the great needs of the community.'[7]

There were signs of improvement in Stoneyburn:

> 'However, new houses have been built by this company at Stoneyburn, which are a great improvement on the type of house hereto-

fore built for the workmen employed in collieries in that district. They are room and kitchen, with scullery, water-closet, coal-cellar, bleaching- and drying-green, garden; also a number with an additional large bedroom (attic). They are well built, well finished, with panelled doors inside. Modern fire grates, water-taps, sink, and washhouses. They are being eagerly sought after by the workmen.'[8]

I sincerely hope that my grandparents were among the successful seekers for one of these new houses; they had eight children in Stoneyburn between 1913 and 1933.

The history, extent and impact of mining in Scotland has been extraordinary, transformational and in some regards, dreadful. There is hardly a town or village in the Scottish Lowlands (and in some parts of the Highlands also) which has not been mined – for coal, shale, iron, lead, zinc, copper, silver and gold. Tens of thousands of men, women and children worked in mining, and it has been estimated that at the beginning of the 20th century, almost one million Scots were directly or indirectly dependent on the industry. Coal fuelled the Industrial Revolution, iron made the machinery that drove it and the railways that transported its products. Modernity depended as much upon mining as it did upon the Enlightenment.

But it also contains within it the most egregious example of what was effectively near slavery, the system of bonded labour whereby coal miners and their families were bound to the colliery in which they worked, and to the service of their owner. In the 17th and 18th centuries, as more forests were cut down and wood became less available as domestic fuel, the commercial value of coal increased well beyond its previous limited use in salt making, and experienced colliers became subject to a kind of bidding war, by which they were induced to move to new collieries. Existing owners, their noses put out of joint, appealed to the Scottish Parliament, which duly legislated on the matter:

'*This bondage was set into law by an Act of Parliament in 1606, which ordained that "no person should fee, hire or conduce and salters, colliers or coal bearers without a written authority from the master whom they had last served". A collier lacking such written authority could be "reclaimed" by his former master "within a year and a day". If the new master did not surrender the collier, he could be fined and the collier who deserted was considered to be a thief and punished accordingly. The Act also gave the coal owners and masters the powers to apprehend "vagabonds and sturdy beggars" and put them to work in the mines. A further Act of 1641 extended those enslaved to include other workers in the mines and forced the colliers to work six days a week.*'[9]

'*Even the Habeas Corpus Act of Scotland, in 1701, which declared that "the imprisonment of persons without expressing the reasons thereof, and delaying to put them to trial is contrary to law"; and that "no person shall hereafter be imprisoned for custody in order to take his trial for any crime or offence without a warrant or writ expressing the particular cause for which he is imprisoned" expressly declared "that this present Act is in no way to be extended to colliers and salters".*'[10]

It was not until 1799 that an Act of Parliament was passed freeing all colliers in Scotland from their servitude. A 1775 Act had made provision for their eventual freeing according to their age, but requiring a kind of time sentence to be served first. These ranged from three to ten years, with the longest time to be served by those between 21 and 34 (the most productive labouring years), allowing the masters to extract every last advantage from the system of bondage. (This process was remarkably similar to the one which ended chattel slavery in the Caribbean some years later.) And since gaining freedom required a formal legal application before a Sheriff, a large number of colliers were still bound until the 1799 Act gave them their full liberation.

The lofty ideals of the Enlightenment, much like the lofty ideals of ancient Greece, only applied in certain circumstances and to certain classes of people, and very rarely indeed when they conflicted with the interests of the landed, the wealthy and the capitalist owners. A concrete instance of this is afforded in a letter by the fourth Earl of Wemyss, an extensive coal-owner in Fife at that time, which was written to his factor in 1751. In requiring him to bring back *'stragled coalliers'*, he says: *'The moment a coallier leaves his work, he ought to be sent after immediately, otherwise it gives him time to gett into England, where he can never be recovered ... Beside the coalliers, their children should be all look't after, and sett to work below ground when capable, and not allow'd to hirr'd cattle or go to service, as many of them have done, and I wish may not be the case as yett. And if you see it for my benefitt and that there's work and room for more people below ground, why don't you gett some of Balbirny's coalliers, who are now in different parts of the country and nobody's property? Pray, are Alexander Leslie's and Thomas Lumsden's children now working at the coal-work?'* [11]

There were numerous ways in which more profit could be squeezed from miners and their families, even after the 1799 Act. One of these was the 'truck' system, also known as the 'company store' system, whereby employees were forced to take all or part of their wages in goods purchased at a store owned by the company. Since there was then no competition to lower prices, which were often artificially high, while the quality of the goods was often inferior, the workers were immediately disadvantaged in this monopoly situation. The company store system was common in mining communities everywhere; probably its most famous depiction is found in *Germinal*, the novel by the French realist Émile Zola, usually considered his masterpiece, which tells the story of striking coal miners in Northern France in the 1860s, and of the harsh conditions and brutality which brought about the strike.

The variant of this system in Scottish mining communities lay particularly in the way in which workers were paid. In many parts of the country, pay-days were fortnightly or monthly, or even sometimes six-weekly, in arrears. Since many, especially those with large families, could not stretch their wages to cover the basics over the longer periods, it was necessary for them to seek advances on their pay. These were readily available, but at a cost – either by a deduction of 6d (penny) to 1s (sterling) in the pound (a 50% deduction) or on the condition that the larger part of the advance, commonly 75%, would be spent in the more expensive company store. The result of this was that many workers found themselves in permanent debt bondage. Refusal to spend the advance in the company store routinely led to the refusal of further advances, and very often to the workers being blacklisted or losing their jobs altogether. Effectively, the stores were supported by those who were compelled to use them.

In some collieries, workmen were obliged to rent houses from the company, whether they needed a house or not. They were also required to pay a deduction for the cost of the company doctor, and Roman Catholics had to pay for their schoolteacher. Though the Truck Act of 1831 made much of this practice illegal, in reality, miners did not have the money to raise civil proceedings against its violation, and were afraid of losing their jobs by raising criminal cases. Miners had no security at all against this system and the abuses attached to it.

I have always been aware of the long mining history in my mother's family. Discovering that one of my paternal great-great-grandfathers, **James Orr**, who I knew was a grocer in Netherton in the west of Glasgow, was actually a company store grocer for the old Netherton Colliery, led to a somewhat anguished family conversation. The truck system has many resonances with what we call today the 'Poverty Premium'.

The Poverty Premium is the additional cost for essential goods and services accruing to people living in poverty as a result of their low incomes. Markets are currently failing to serve people who are already struggling to make ends meet. It is a basic injustice that the poorest end up paying more than wealthier citizens for everyday essentials such as food: the rising cost of food is a particular problem for low-income households, who have less disposable income to spend on food. Food is often more expensive in poorer areas where access to big supermarkets is limited. The Poverty Premium affects fuel: low-income households pay higher-than-average prices for gas and electricity. Households who use prepayment meters pay on average £253 more per year than those who pay by direct debit. Finance too: excluded from mainstream credit, people on low incomes are reliant on high-cost credit offered by doorstep or payday lenders, frequently charging interest rates in excess of 1000% APR. And with little or no savings or access to cheap credit, people have no option other than to purchase furniture and household appliances from 'rent-to-own' companies. Former Market leader Bright-House (which went into administration in 2020) charged almost four times the price of the identical goods bought elsewhere. And perhaps the final indignity, today what used to be known as 'pauper's funerals' have returned; with affordable options not available or properly advertised, people often pay more than they can afford for funerals.

The cost of the Poverty Premium to low-income families can be up to £1500 a year. Every one of these essential needs was subject to the same Poverty Premium in the 19th-century truck system operating in hundreds of collieries. While one part of my family struggled under harsh conditions to make ends meet, it seems that another part may well have been exploiting the extreme precariousness and vulnerability of very poor workers.

If that was indeed the case, it served James Orr and his family well. A farmer's son himself, he and his wife Agnes were raising a family which was establishing itself within the ranks of respectable tradespeople (and gradually accumulating the prosperity to enable all the six children of his second son James, my great-grandfather, to join the professional, university-educated middle class). Their three daughters were all dressmakers. Their eldest son was a master joiner. Their second son was a provisions merchant, with a grocer's shop in various premises in Glasgow city centre. Their fourth son was also a master grocer. Their third son, an engine-fitter, died tragically by drowning after falling off Finnieston Quay at the age of 20. On the wall of a disgracefully neglected graveyard in Maryhill, a wall tablet erected by his grieving parents commemorates his death.

***

James Lamond, Clement Johnston and James Orr were not my only great-great-grandfathers involved in the mining industry, however. Another ended up there by a rather different route. **Maurice Morrin** was born in Ireland in 1829. By 1853, he was living in Bonhill in the Vale of Leven in West Dunbartonshire. Did he come from one of the Irish weaving counties with skills to get him work in the developing textile industry in Bonhill, or more likely, as part of the great wave of Irish migration into Scotland in the wake of the Irish famine of 1846-47? We don't know. Bonhill was only five miles from Cardross, where John Fleming was the Head Gardener. And indeed, by 1855, Maurice too was working in Cardross, as a coachman at Cardross House, the other 'big house' in the area. Cardross is not a large place; I like to imagine that my great-great-grandfathers might have known each other. But Maurice's working life and prospects were less settled than John's. In 1861, he was a coachman at the elegant, Robert Adam-designed Langside House, Cathcart (now part of Glasgow). By 1865, he was driving omnibuses in Glasgow, and by 1881, he too had moved eastwards to West Calder, four miles from Stoneyburn, and was working as a coal pithead labourer. At the time of his death there in 1894, he was recorded as a lodging-house keeper, providing accommodation for Irish immigrants.

Over on the Ayrshire west coast, meanwhile, the farming Campbells were being fruitful and multiplying mightily. **John Campbell**, the great-great-grandson of Andrew Campbell, born in 1806, was now farming at Knockjarder, overlooking Dalrymple Church, in whose churchyard he is buried. He was farming 225 acres, quite a substantial spread – which is just as well, for he had many people to support from it. John married four times. His first wife died just fifteen months after their marriage; their only child died five days after her mother. He and his second wife, Marion Farquhar, a 29-year-old widow with two children, had another 11 children. After Marion died in 1867, he married twice more – his last wife was 27 years his junior.

John then moved to Low Milton Farm, just outside Maybole, another large farm which employed five people, where he was a well-known and well-respected farmer and a regular contributor at public talks, agricultural shows and in newspaper articles. Had he been there twenty years earlier, he might have known **John Thomson** (whose great-granddaughter would marry his own great-grandson in Edinburgh a century later), who married Elizabeth Aitken in Maybole in 1852 at the age of 22. But probably not; though they lived within a few miles of each other, Dalrymple being only 4.5 miles from Maybole, and both worked in agriculture, they inhabited different social and economic positions. John Thomson is described in the few biographical details we know of him as a ploughman, a pig farmer and a carter. In 1852, he was working as a farm servant in Kirkoswald, four miles south of Maybole. Farm servants were the third group of people working in agriculture in Lowland Scotland during the 19th century, and the lowest in social status, at the base of the triangle of tenant farmers, who employed them, and the landowners to whom the farms ultimately belonged. They were landless farm workers, with little or no expectation of ever being tenant farmers themselves, much less of owning land, at a time when the trend was moving in the opposite direction from small subsistence farming towards much larger farms, aggregating smallholdings into ventures able to make a profit.

John Thomson may have been taken on at one of the annual hiring fairs, contracted for a set period, perhaps three years, and accommodated in a farm cottage along with his family. Certainly, his first son was born in Kirkoswald, six months after his parents' wedding. But by 1854, this young family was on the move again, first to Ayr, then to Glasgow in 1856. Less than ten years after his marriage, John had died before the age of thirty, leaving his widow with five children under eight.

The trajectory followed thereafter by the descendants of these two men, John Thomson and John Campbell, is very different. Thomas Thomson, my great-grandfather, joined the eastward move from Glasgow to West Lothian, becoming a coal miner in Woodmuir and eventually a carter in Stoneyburn, where all his six sons also became miners. Henry Campbell, also my great-grandfather, the seventh generation of his family to be born in Dalrymple, farmed for some years at High Pinmore Farm in Maybole. But by the 1880s, when he was still a young man, he moved north and west, and, described as a *'retired'* farmer, he was living in Albert Park, the handsome villa in Kilcreggan on the Rosneath Peninsula. From there, having married into money, he produced a family for the British Empire.

***

But where did the money come from? The answer to that question lies with the last of my great-great-grandfathers, **Adam McLellan**. Born in Inchinnan, near Paisley, in 1819, the son of a Glasgow joiner, Adam made his living as a clothier and hatter. In her fascinating book *Payback: Debt and the Shadow Side of Wealth*, Margaret Atwood quotes a 17th-century proverb: *'Put a miller, a weaver and a tailor together in a bag and shake them, and the first one that comes out will be a thief.'*[12] She attributes the popular belief that all three professions were likely thieves to the fact that none of them grew or made something themselves, but rather were processors of raw materials

– grain, yarn or cloth – whose value addition was hard to quantify, and who were therefore well-placed to cheat or pilfer. Well, primary producers have often lost out to the processors, who have tended to be much better rewarded, and having all three of these professions in my lineage is interesting; especially since there is a little bit of family dubiety around Adam.

A very old family photograph of him, probably taken around 1851, shows an elegant young man in a light-coloured three-piece suit, cravat and high collar, with a cane across his knee, rings on both his pinkies and a side-parting in his long curls. In 1850, he had married Catherine Lyall, the daughter, and sole heir, of George Lyall, a spirit dealer from Paisley. Catherine had six siblings, all but one of whom predeceased their father, who died in 1854, leaving her surviving brother, George Junior, to inherit everything. George, however, tragically for him but perhaps not for Adam McLellan, died as the result of a bite from a rabid dog later the same year. His family's status was significant enough to warrant a Paisley newspaper reporting on the tragedy. And thereby, Adam became a wealthy man, wealthy enough to visit the Paris Exhibition in 1855, to move to Kilcreggan and build a house there, and to retire at the age of fifty-two. It was his daughter Margaret who married Henry Campbell in 1872.

The lives of these eight men, my great-great-grandfathers, span almost the whole of the 19th century, from 1800 when James Orr was born, until 1894, when John Fleming and Maurice Morrin both died. It was a century of enormous social, economic and political change for Scotland, and the change is reflected in all of their lives, for better but also for worse.

For John Campbell, the Ayrshire tenant farmer, the 19th century had seen the consolidation of the 18th-century enclosure of common land, the aggregation of small farms into larger ones and the improvement of agricultural practice. Farming had changed from being mostly subsistence and localised to being an enterprise geared towards markets and income generation. The Campbells were now substantial tenant farmers, with a larger than average acreage, and a household which included both domestic and farm servants. By remaining in one small part of Ayrshire, being, one can infer, respectable and reliable tenants, members of the Church of Scotland, the Established Church, their fortunes were gradually but consistently improving, and almost all of John's very large family in their turn lived and died in the parishes of Dalrymple and Maybole.

For John Thomson, the Agricultural Revolution had not been such a positive experience. It had led to an attack on the cottar system of smallholdings granted in return for labour, and to the widespread dispossession and removal of cottar families from their homes. Tens of thousands were forced either to move to the cities and factories of the burgeoning Industrial Revolution, or into emigration. Others were forced entirely into the waged economy, dependent on selling their labour on short-term contracts. For a man with a family, it was an unsettled and insecure life, and so it proved for John Thomson.

For three of the four men whose livelihoods were dependent on mining, the picture is a very common one – for Lowland Scotland and for mining in general. James Lamond the shale miner, Clement Johnston the joiner and Maurice Morrin the pithead labourer all moved eastward across Central Scotland in stages, sometimes moving only a few miles to where the next employment was. All of them had to turn their hands to different kinds of work, whether underground or above, or in servicing pits and pit villages. All of them had poor housing conditions and amenities. The rights and rewards available to them for their dangerous and unpleasant occupations, notwithstanding its essential importance to their country and people, seem remarkably meagre to the modern view.

For James Orr, the company store grocer, the middleman, on the other hand, the 19th century was one of increased prosperity, and his sons and daughters were able to move away from the coal mine and establish themselves as tradespeople in Glasgow, perhaps encouraged by their redoubtable mother, who was still identifying herself as a grocer in the 1901 census, when she was 93. Adam McLellan, the clothier and tailor with the wealthy wife, was also part of the growth of the increasing merchant class who played such an important role in the development of Glasgow as the 'second city of the Empire'.

As for John Fleming, the only one of these men who was in any way distinguished, and whose achievements are still remembered beyond his family, the famous garden he created and the books he wrote did not bring him economic success. In 1877, while he was still in Cardross, he was declared bankrupt. A notice appeared in the *Edinburgh Gazette*:

> '*SEQUESTRATION of JOHN FLEMING, Senior, Gardener, residing at Kilmahew Cottage, Cardross, Dumbartonshire, as an Individual, and as a Partner of the now dissolved Firm of J. FLEMING & SONS, Seedsmen and Fruiterers, No.12 Charing Cross, Sauchiehall Street, Glasgow.*

> '*PETER. M'NICOLL, Accountant in Glasgow, has been elected Trustee on the Estate; and Thomas Hardie, Ironfounder, Dumbarton, Executor of the late James Anderson Hardie, Engineer and Ironfounder, Dumbarton, James Stewart Saddler, Partner of the Firm of Smith & Simons, Seed Merchants, Glasgow, and George Galloway, Partner of Robertson & Galloway, Seed Merchants and Nurserymen, 157 Ingram Street, Glasgow, and the Hermitage, Helensburgh, have been elected Commissioners. The Examination of the Bankrupt will take place in the Sheriff Court House, Dumbarton, on Tuesday the 22d day of May next, at one o'clock afternoon. The Creditors will meet in the Chambers of Messrs. Girdwood & M'Nicoll, Accountants, 28 Bath Street, Glasgow, on Wednesday the 30th day of May current, at one o'clock afternoon.*

> '*PETER M'NicoLL, Trustee.*
> *Glasgow, 16th May 1877.*'[13]

Two months later, the following notice appeared in the same publication:

> 'PETER M'NICOLL, *Accountant in Glasgow, Trustee on the Sequestrated Estates of* JOHN FLEMING *Senior, Gardener, residing at Kilmahew Cottage, Cardross, Dumbartonshire, as an Individual, and as a Partner of the now dissolved Firm of J. FLEMING & SONS, Seedsmen and Fruiterers, No.12 Charing Cross, Sauchiehall Street, Glasgow, hereby intimates that at the Meeting of Creditors, held upon the 4th day of July last, the Bankrupt offered to the Creditors a Composition on his whole debts of Two Shillings per pound, payable two and four months after his final discharge, with security; and that the Creditors present unanimously entertained said offer for consideration; and Notice is hereby given that it will be decided upon at a Meeting of the Creditors, to be held within the Counting House of Girdwood & M'Nicoll, Accountants, No.28 Bath Street, Glasgow, upon Friday the 27th day of July 1877, at one o'clock afternoon.*
>
> '*PETER M 'NicoLL, Trustee.*
> *Glasgow, 18th July 1877.*'[14]

It is not hard to imagine that this bankruptcy and its public nature would have been a humiliation for John Fleming. Perhaps, in a time before old-age pensions, he was looking for a business that would provide for him and his large family. He was, after all, nearing sixty, and ultimately, only a servant. After twenty-five years, he left Kilmahew, moved to Glasgow and is recorded in the 1881 census as a cemetery superintendent, and in the 1891 census as a greengrocer. His wife had had to go into domestic service at the age of nearly sixty, presumably to help repay the creditors. For all of these men, in this century of rupture, dislocation and improvement, some hard facts remained – without land or capital, upward mobility and economic improvement were almost impossible, and trade, even in this mercantile century, was still a very risky business.

Notes:

1. John Fleming, *Wild Flowers in the West of Scotland*, Alex Malcolm, 1880

2. Edwin Morgan, poem written for the opening of the Scottish Parliament, 9 October, 2004. Contains information licensed under the Scottish Parliament Copyright Licence

3. ibid. 2

4. From *The Industries of Scotland: Their Rise, Progress, and Present Condition*, by David Bremner, A. and C. Black, Edinburgh, 1869

5. ibid. 4

6. Evidence given by Robert Hood, Chairman of the Scottish Shale Miners' Association; Robert Small, General Secretary of the Shale Miners' Association; and Theodore K Irvine, Architect and Builder, attending, advising as experts to the Scottish Shale Miners' Association to the Royal Commission on Housing

7. ibid. 6

8. Evidence given by Robert Brown, representative of the Mid and East Lothian Miners' Association

9. From the Scottish Mining website: www.scottishmining.co.uk

10. From *Flying Shots: Or Contributions to the Periodical Press*, William Hutchison, A. Fullarton and Co., Edinburgh, London and Dublin, 1852

11. From *Chamber's Journal*, 1894

12. Margaret Atwood, *Payback: Debt and the Shadow Side of Wealth*, 2008, CBC Massey Lectures, House of Anansi Press

13. *Edinburgh Gazette* accessed via www.findmypast.com

14. *Edinburgh Gazette* accessed via www.findmypast.com

About the mothers, 1800-1900

She maun labour frae sunrise till dark,
An' aft tho' her means be but sma',
She gets little thanks for her wark –
Or as aften gets nae thanks ava.
She maun tak just whatever may come,
An' say nocht o' her fear or her hope;
There's nae use o' lievin' in Rome,
And tryin' to fecht wi' the Pope.
Hectored an' lectured an a',
Snubbed for whate'er may befa',
Than this, she is far better aff –
That never gets married ava.

(Joanna Picken)[1]

I am a feminist, by which I mean someone who believes in the equal
status and value of women, advocates for equal rights and responsibilities for women, and seeks measures that redress imbalances of
well-being, livelihood, health and education for women. Why am I
a feminist? Let me put it this way. When I was a teenager:

- *it was legal to pay women less than men for doing exactly the*
  same job;
- *it was legal to discriminate against women in employment, voca-*
  tional training, education and the provision of goods and services;
- *it was legal to exclude women from a wide range of occupations,*
  premises and activities because they were women;
- *it was legal for a woman to be forced to resign from her job if she*
  got married;
- *it was legal for a woman to have to obtain her husband's written*
  consent to open a bank account or take out a mortgage;
- *it was legal for a man to rape his wife;*

- *it was illegal for a woman to have an abortion for any reason whatsoever.*

All of these things have changed, in Britain at least. I am proud to have been part of the movement that brought about these changes. I am, and always will be, proud to call myself a feminist. I am of course a woman of my time and culture, and formed in part by the society I grew up and have lived in. But I am also formed by the values, attitudes and practices of my own family, as they had been by theirs. So, I am interested in the experiences of my forefathers, and particularly of my foremothers. What was it like for them being women from a variety of backgrounds in Scotland?

I was born in the middle of the 20th century, a baby boomer, into a loving, not well-off but very secure extended family, in the rural south-west of Scotland. I have spent a lifetime since then discovering just how privileged that makes me, part of a generation perhaps more secure than any before or since. It has given me good health, free health care, free primary, secondary and higher education, social mobility, access to the arts, political engagement, travel, beauty and opportunity. If I die tomorrow, my life will still have been longer, freer and fuller of possibility than the vast majority of women in history, including now – and including every one of my female ancestors.

Like their husbands, the eight women who were my great-great-grandmothers had lives which also spanned the 19th century: from Marion Farquhar, who was born in 1802, to **Agnes Hamilton**, who, born in 1806, actually lived into the 20th century, dying in 1903 at the age of 96 – an enormously long lifespan for a woman of her time and class. Agnes was the daughter of James Hamilton, cattle dealer, and Agnes Wilson, and she was born in Glassford, a small village near the county town of Hamilton. The landed family in the area, then and now, also bore the Hamilton name and were among the many Scots aristocracy who owed their patrimony to Robert the Bruce (having cannily changed sides following the Battle of

Bannockburn). However, Agnes's branch of the family was landless and poor, and she married James Orr the grocer at the age of twenty-three in Glasgow. Soon they had moved to Netherton, just outside the western edge of the city, to run the company store at Netherton Colliery. Agnes and James had seven children, all of whom became established in trades in Netherton and Glasgow, with the sad exception of the son who drowned.

Perhaps the most interesting story surrounds the women of the family. Agnes herself outlived all of her sons, but continued to run the original family business after their deaths, even though she was by now well into old age. Her three daughters, Agnes, Jane and Janet, all became dressmakers with their own business, and Agnes and Jane, neither of whom married, continued to work together after the marriage of Janet to Alexander Dunlop in 1872. However, this brother-in-law does not seem to have been much loved by the sisters.

In 1904, the year after her mother died, Agnes made a will. With both her parents and all her brothers now dead, the three sisters had inherited their equal share of the movable estate. There is no record of any heritable estate (that is, land or property, which would in any case have gone to the oldest son and then to his heirs), but there was certainly sufficient money, furniture and other movable possessions to warrant the making of a will. Agnes's estate left over £1200, worth about £112,000 today (and worth considerably more in terms of her economic and social status). Jane, as a mature single woman, would have been in charge of her own money, and so, theoretically, should Janet have been, since the Married Women's Property Act of 1881 had given back to married women the right to own and control their own property. Before then, a woman's property automatically became the property of her husband upon marriage.

That there was still some tension around this is evident in Agnes's will, in which she bequeathed £400 to Jane, £400 to Janet and Janet's daughter Nettie, £300 to Janet's son Alexander and another £100 to another nephew, James Orr. But in making these bequests, Agnes writes dismissively and forcefully: *'her [Janet's] husband to have nothing to do with it'*. In the event, Janet died before Agnes in 1907, and Agnes and Jane continued to live together in Netherton till 1909, when they died within ten days of each other. Jane, who died after Agnes, wrote her own will on her deathbed in the Western Infirmary the day before she died, where it was witnessed by the physician who attended her there. She left her similarly substantial estate to six nieces, four nephews, and the second largest bequest to the wife of one of the nephews in her own right.

Clearly these two hard-working sisters, who lived together in Netherton their whole lives and died more or less simultaneously, had no intention of allowing any of their or their family's hard-earned money to go to Janet's husband, though they were generous to Janet's children. Was Alexander Dunlop spendthrift while they carefully saved their earnings? Was he lazy, a trait which would have not endeared him to women who, like their mother, had never been idle? Or does this suggest something more malign? Who can tell; but there was clearly no love lost between the sisters and their brother-in-law, in a wider family which was characterised by close relationships and mutual support. The disposition of their estates, and hence the importance of making a will, was one of the few ways for women to exercise economic agency at a time when almost the whole of women's lives was controlled by men. But the extent of their estates makes it obvious that by this time, the Orr family had moved firmly into the Glasgow merchant middle class, and that in the course of her long 19th century, Agnes had seen her family move far from her own poor agricultural background and away from the mining company store, and her daughters in particular become independent and successful businesswomen.

***

Wills, and the making of them, was of supreme importance to another great-great-grandmother, **Catherine Lyall**. Born in 1827, the daughter of George Lyall, a wealthy Paisley wine and spirit merchant and his wife Catherine McGregor, she was the third of seven children, including two brothers. She would hardly have expected to be the sole heir of her father, and yet the untimely deaths of all her siblings meant that, in 1859, Catherine inherited what was by the standards of the time, a large fortune. By this time, Catherine had married Adam McLellan, a Glasgow clothier, and borne two daughters to him. But in the 1850s, when a woman married, all her wealth and property immediately became the possession of her husband.

The story of Adam and Catherine – of their unhappy marriage and Adam's life and adventures as a man of property, of the building of a house that remains a mystery, and of Catherine's ultimate tragic death – continues in another chapter. But it's a salutary reminder that riches were no guarantee of security or happiness for a woman in 19th-century Scotland.

Worries about wills and inheritances did not figure in the lives of my two (unrelated) Aitken great-great-grandmothers. They had enough other worries. **Janet Aitken** was born in Kirkintilloch on January 1, 1831 to Robert Aitken and Janet Freebairn, the fourth of nine children. Most of her siblings had unremarkable and common names; three of her sisters were called respectively, Elizabeth, Margaret and Isabella, and they are not recorded as having middle names. But the oldest sister had the rather exotic name of Annrietta Stirling Gray Aitken. This is such an unlikely name for the daughter of a cotton handloom weaver, when Scottish tradition would call the oldest daughter after her maternal grandmother, that it is likely that she was named instead for a daughter of the local laird, William Gray, who married the son of Sir John Stirling, who had opened the first cotton mill in Scotland in Kirkintilloch. Perhaps her mother had been in domestic service with the Gray family. By the 1841 census, she appears as Ann, perhaps an easier name to live with. Janet and at least three of her siblings were, like their father, cotton handloom weavers from an early age – in Janet's case, from the age of 10.

Handloom weaving was still a major domestic industry, and cotton particularly so in the West of Scotland. In 1790, there were 185 handloom weavers in Kirkintilloch. Since the 18th century, textiles had been the largest manufacturing industry in Scotland by a long way, and even by 1830, it is estimated that over a quarter of a million Scots worked in cotton, linen and wool, over 60% in cotton alone. The majority of these were still engaged in family and home-based production. Janet's family certainly looks like a work unit. It's not clear whether they had a small piece of land but if they did, it certainly was not large enough to support all their needs, so the handloom weaving was a common way of generating income. Robert Aitken's father was a tailor, so the cloth trade was familiar to them. It was a hard way of life, with long hours and health hazards; Robert himself died of asthma, a common illness for people who worked in the textile industry. But domestic handloom weaving did allow a small degree of autonomy and control; importantly, as increasingly weaving became mechanised and more people moved to factories as waged labour, the family business allowed any profits to be retained by the workers rather than by the factory owners.

For women too, domestic handloom weaving was somewhat more equitable and less gender-differentiated. Though handloom weavers were mostly men, many wives and daughters worked alongside their husbands and fathers, and eventually women also worked as outworkers on piecework contracts. The move to the factories and power loom production was also a move to lower wages for women. Being a weaver was seen as a skilled artisanal trade, and increasingly women were excluded from weaving jobs in factories in order to maintain wage differentials favouring men.

This process was well under way by the time Janet married James Lamond in 1851. James was a miner from Greenock, and over the next 20 years, they moved from pit to pit in Kilwinning, in Kirkintilloch and eventually to the shale mines in West Calder. During these years, Janet gave birth to two daughters and five sons. One of her sons died in infancy; the others all followed their father down the shale mines, and her daughters both went into domestic service. She died at the age of 51 from tuberculosis, one of the many of my family, and everybody else's family, to do so.

***

My other Aitken great-great-grandmother, **Elizabeth Aitken**, came from Irvine in Ayrshire, the daughter of James Aitken, a gardener, and Katherine Laverty, whose name suggests Irish origins. Katherine died when Elizabeth was born, leaving Elizabeth and her two-year-old sister Nancy motherless. The following year, James Aitken remarried, and he and his second wife had six more children. In 1852, Elizabeth married the Kirkoswald farm servant John Thomson when she was already three months pregnant. By 1861, she had five children, and her young husband was dead.

In a pattern that is all too familiar among the 19th-century poor, for whom raising a family and earning a living at the same time were all but impossible alone, Elizabeth was partnered again in a year with William Murray, a Glasgow grain miller with whom she had another three children. But before she was sixty, she was once more alone, and with her children grown, needing to support herself. She worked as a laundress in Glasgow; then at the age of 73, she is recorded as being an outdoor worker – hard work for a woman of her age – living back in Maybole, where she had married as a young woman. She died in 1901 of cirrhosis of the liver; it is not hard to see how the facts of her hard life might have caused her to take refuge in the bottle.

***

Of all my great-great-grandmothers, **Mary Wilson** was the one with the deepest roots in coal mining. She was the daughter and the sister of miners; she became the wife and mother of miners also. Her birthplace, the small town of Polmont in the county of Stirling, had three collieries within its parish bounds, the largest of which, the Redding Colliery, belonged to our old friend the Duke of Hamilton. At the time of Mary's birth in 1820, it was being extensively worked, and according to the Statistical Accounts of Scotland in 1845, the Redding Colliery and its near neighbour, the Middlerigg Colliery, employed between them upwards of 400 men-miners, labourers and artificers – as well as drawers, a role usually performed by boys or women and girls.

The employment of women and children in the mines was a subject of considerable controversy. The work done by women and children was backbreaking in the extreme. The drawers carried or pushed or pulled heavy loads of coal from the coalface to the surface, frequently weighing well over a hundredweight (112 lbs or 50 kgs), some reported carrying or pushing or pulling up to 8 hundredweights. Average shifts were twelve hours, mostly below ground in almost complete darkness, many were longer. Children as young as seven were employed in filling the carts, hewing the coal was done by boys from about ten onwards, and sometimes by women, mostly widows who were breadwinners for their families. The Scottish Mining Website carries detailed reports from the Children's Employment Commission of 1842; one from Redding Colliery offers a description by the colliery's manager which confirms the employment of women and children in considerable numbers, paints an optimistic picture of the educational opportunities available for the children, but effectively washes its hands of any responsibility of the employer for the use of child labour, stating that they do not interfere in the use of child labour, which is at the discretion of the colliers themselves.

Reading the testimonies of the women and children themselves gives a somewhat different perspective. The wealthy men who owned these mines and enjoyed the comforts, luxuries and influence available to those who could afford them were enabled to do so by women doing hard labour of the kind we associate with Siberian gulags and Louisiana prison-camps, and by primary-school-age children crawling through mud in the dark for twelve hours at a time. They strike me as utterly despicable, and a disgrace to any religion they claimed to adhere to.

A combination of public pressure and the desire of employers to gain more control over the labour force led to the passing of the Mines Act of 1842, in order *'to prohibit the Employment of Women and Girls in Mines and Collieries, to regulate the Employment of Boys, and make Provisions for the Safety of Persons working therein'.*[2] But there was a degree of ambivalence about the Act, similar in many ways to what happens today in efforts to halt child labour globally. With the best of intentions, such legislation can only be really effective if it addresses causes and not symptoms. The banning of women and young children from the mines did not answer the question of how lone women, especially those with children to support, in a country with no social security or welfare, might find alternative sources of income. It would take someone deeply cynical to believe that parents put their children into such appalling conditions for any reason other than desperation; the fact that so many children routinely pulled a twelve-hour shift of hard labour and then went to school at night rather suggests a recognition and valuing of education, even in the worst circumstances.

But desperate and sometimes destitute women whose whole lives had been lived in mining communities saw their livelihoods, such as they were, being taken away, with nothing to replace them. The Scottish Mining Website has numerous petitions from or written on behalf of such women in advance of the passing of the Act, requesting that at the very least, single women and widows should be exempted from its regulations. However, there are also counter-petitions, from coal miners who were of the view that *'if the employment of femails above eighteen years of age were not more profitable to the employers of Fifeshire and the Lothians, than to the femails themselves, their Petitions would not be so well nor so ready got up.*

'Your Petitioners are prepared to prove that Petitions have been got up in coal works wholily at the instance of the employers, in favour of the femails being kept in the pits, as also it is plain the employers would have complied with the Act in November last, had it not been that they are large profiters by such an inhumain systum.'[3]

Men were in support of the Act but also wanted the women removed because they worked for lower wages than the men. It's not hard to sympathise with both points of view. But though the Act did eventually get the women and young children away from their inhuman and degrading work in the mines, many of the industrial and social trends emerging in the mid-19th century were not always helpful for women. Increasingly, the work that men did, especially if they were skilled workers, was being redesignated as 'breadwinner' work – and the breadwinner was always understood to be the man. Therefore, they needed higher wages in order to support a family. Never mind that many households were headed by widows, or that many single people also needed to make a living, which might include supporting elderly or sick relatives. The male head of the household became normative, and, as with textiles, they required work that was seen as higher status and better paid than women's work. To have a wife who did not work became a mark of masculinity and morality.

In order to justify the reduced participation of women in the labour force, where they might compete for jobs, and where employers could undercut male wages by paying women less, reasons had to be found to exclude them – that they were too weak and frail, that their proper place was in the home, that dependency was their natural state. The division of labour into men's work (the 'real' work) and women's work (the domestic) was well under way, with consequences that remain today.

***

That manager at the Redding Colliery was my great-great-great-grandfather, John Johnston, and it was his son, Clement Johnston, whom Mary Wilson married in 1847. Clement was a skilled man, who worked as a millwright and engineer in Polmont and nearby Slamannan, eventually settling in Woodmuir and Addiewell, where he worked as a joiner. Mary and Clement had three daughters and three sons, two of whom worked in mining. At least one of their daughters, Mary, went into service.

Becoming a domestic servant was increasingly an option for women workers, and by 1851, a third of them were servants. There were both push and pull factors in this movement. In rural areas, the agricultural changes that saw farms increasingly consolidated into larger tenancies and holdings meant that many former farm servants moved to urban areas looking for work. Domestic industry such as handloom weaving was declining in the face of industrialisation, and job demarcation meant that industrial occupations were increasingly gendered, often to protect male wages. The growth of a much larger middle class, adding artisan, mercantile and trading, and white-collar employment to the formerly small professional middle class, meant that there were many more households who wished to employ servants. And the increasing confinement of women to the domestic 'separate sphere' meant that work for poor women was most readily available in the homes of better-off women. Being able to keep a servant, or servants, became one of the most visible forms of class identification. It was a sign of middle-class respectability.

But though service paid better than other jobs, since it usually included room and board, it was hardly the *Downton Abbey* television fantasy. The work was mostly sheer drudgery, the hours were very long – twelve to fourteen hours a day – and there was little privacy and less independence, with personal life as well as working life under the control of employers. For **Ann Miller**, going into service must have been a bitter pill to swallow. Married to the

Cardross master gardener John Fleming, she had lived in a substantial lodge house on the Kilmahew Estate, and there raised a family of eight children. This daughter of a farmer turned coal miner had herself employed a servant. But in 1877, her husband had been declared bankrupt after the seed business he had started with his sons had failed. The family had moved from Cardross to Glasgow, where Ann, by now a grandmother, was recorded in her death certificate in 1880 as a domestic servant, aged 58. Presumably she was doing this in order to help pay off the family debts.

***

The service industry was not limited to live-in or household domestic work. The only one of my great-great-grandmothers who did not come from the west or central Lowlands was **Marrion Gilchrist**, born in 1824 in Islay, the most southerly of the Inner Hebrides. Marrion was one of the nine children of Mary McGregor and Archibald Gilchrist, the schoolmaster (and registrar) in the parish of Kilchoman in the west of Islay. The island, whose population had grown considerably through the second half of the 18th century, had around 15,000 inhabitants by 1830, but the agriculture and fishing which were the mainstay of its economy had hit hard times. Collapsing markets after the end of the Napoleonic Wars, the same kinds of agricultural changes which had taken place in the Lowlands which removed smallholders from their land and replaced them with much larger sheep farms, and finally the spread of the potato blight from nearby Ireland, all meant that the island could not support its population, and many faced destitution. Many islanders had already emigrated, to the USA and particularly to Canada, over the previous hundred years, and men and women had been leaving Islay for Glasgow and the Lowlands, to farm labour and domestic service, but now the stream became a flood. Marrion and several of her siblings were among them.

At first Marrion worked as a laundress in the service of the

Dennistoun family of Golfhill House, another prominent Glasgow family with strong links to plantation slavery. By 1853, she was living in Largs, on the Ayrshire coast, presumably in service there. She had also somewhere met Maurice Morrin, the Irish migrant, and they married in Largs, and moved to Strathblane, 16 miles away on the other side of the Kilpatrick Hills. It was here that their first child, my great-grandmother, was born in 1854. Here is another child whose full name is intriguing; she was christened Sarah Wallis Smith Morrin, but neither of her middle names appear in either parent's families. It's very likely that Maurice was the coachman of William Smith, a wealthy West Indies merchant and plantation owner, who later became Lord Provost of Glasgow, whose estate in Strathblane was called Carbeth Guthrie. William's wife was an Irish woman from County Cork, and her name was Sarah Wallis Smith. Might the Irish coachman and his Hebridean wife have named their first child after their employer's wife, out of respect or hope of favour, or in a small gesture of Celtic solidarity?

In the next eight years, Marrion and Maurice had moved again, first to Cardross, he still working as a coachman, and where their next two children, Peter and Duncan, named after Marrion's brothers, were born, and then to Cathcart, where Maurice was an omnibus driver, and where their last child, Andrew, was born. In 1865, at the age of 39, Marrion Gilchrist, the schoolmaster's daughter from a remote rural parish in Islay, died in Glasgow of tuberculosis, leaving four children under eleven.

Maurice then lived with another Highland woman, Mary McKellar from Kilmichael Glassary, gradually moving east to the mining areas of West Lothian, and finally settled as a lodging-house keeper in West Calder, where he and Mary had a household of ten boarders, all men and mostly labourers from Ireland. He died in 1894. Doubtless this was hard graft for Mary, but taking in boarders was an accepted way of increasing household income and making a virtue out of necessity as women were increasingly confined to the domestic sphere.

Taking in boarders reoccurs regularly in my family. Elizabeth Aitken, the young widow of John Thomson, married her lodger William Murray (or perhaps he was her bidie-in). After their move to Glasgow and the death of his wife, and in the scramble to pay off his creditors, John Fleming lived in a flat in Gibson Street with two of his sons and his daughter Grace, and their lodger, a medical student at nearby Glasgow University. After John's remarriage in 1881, Grace moved to live with her sister Eliza, now married to James Orr, the brother of the redoubtable Agnes (and personal beneficiary in Jane Orr's will), and their six children, plus a Japanese engineering student, in a house later demolished to make way for the Boyd Orr building in the University. She lived with them for the rest of her life. When I was a child, we had in our house a small crystal mug (presumably a christening mug) engraved with the words 'Grace Fleming 1844', and I used to drink out of it, and wonder about Grace Fleming who had lived more than a century before me. My grandmother explained to me that she was my Grandpa's aunt, but my Grandpa had died before I was born, and it all seemed unimaginably remote to me then.

This was clearly not just a working-class occupation. Adam McLellan's sister Elizabeth kept a lodging house in Sandbank Buildings, on the west side of Clyde Street, where her household in 1871 included two Irish marine draughtsmen and an engine fitter with his family. And Margaret McLellan Campbell, my great-grandmother, the mistress of Albert Park, was also taking in boarders and letting rooms, both in Albert Park and in Glasgow. From 1881 until 1907, Mrs Campbell was advertising *'bedrooms/sitting-room, with attendance, in a house prettily situated, with splendid views'*, or, in 1907, *'room with board to let for the winter'*, or, in 1903, *'the whole house to let for the summer months – 3 public, 5 bedrooms, kitchen, scullery &c; large garden, coach house and stable'*. After her husband Henry's death in 1896, Margaret had taken a large flat in the West End of Glasgow, where she was living with three of her children and two French language teachers from Germany and Switzerland. This resourceful widow maintained two establishments, one in Glasgow and one in the somewhat inaccessible but very pretty village of Kilcreggan, by dint of running them both as letting or boarding houses.

***

But the great-great-grandmother who undoubtedly had the largest household was **Marion Farquhar**. Oh, Marion, what can I say about you? That you were the tenth and youngest child of a farming family in Kirkmichael, a few miles from Dalrymple. That your mother was 45 when you were born, and lived to the age of 71. That when you were 22, you married a young exciseman, James Christie, and had two children with him. That within seven years, he was dead, and you had returned to Dalrymple to marry John Campbell, a widower four years your junior, whose first wife had died giving birth to a daughter who also died. That in your blended family, you gave birth to another eleven children, the last when you were 46, three of whom died in infancy. That your oldest child Robert, your son with James, died aged 18 in Tobago in the West Indies. That your household included both domestic and farm servants-labourers, ploughmen and byre maids, never less than a dozen to feed every day. That as the farmer's wife in a sizeable arable and dairy farm, you would have been responsible for the cheese and butter production, for home consumption and for sale, milking at 5am, and again at 7pm – the hours were long, the routine never-ending, and never a moment in the day when there was not some task, animal or child needing to be attended to.

Of course, most married women in the 19th century had many more children than most women in Scotland today do, though even then, Marion's family was large. Their birth rate was high for the same reasons that it still is for women today in many parts of the world. Some families, perhaps particularly those in agriculture, needed children to provide their labour force without having to pay wages to hired-in workers. In a time when there was no social security, and only poor relief or the dreaded workhouse in times of hardship and destitution, people depended on their children, siblings relied on their siblings and adult children relied on their extended families for assistance in age, illness, unemployment or with childcare. They also looked for work opportunities through family businesses, trade or skills-related closed-shops, or any recommendations, introductions or openings that family connections could offer. Those people and media in wealthy countries who today display outrage and disdain at what they declare to be corruption, graft or nepotism in poor countries might usefully remember that until the middle of the 20th century, this was the way things were done in this country as well, doubtless by their own families too. Families were not just personal security; they were social security. Some elements of this are fast returning in the UK in our own era of increasing inequality.

But it wasn't just as a kind of lifetime insurance that women gave birth so regularly and indeed incessantly. Child mortality was far higher in Scotland than it is now. Of the 55 children my 8 great-great-grandmothers bore, 7 died at birth or in infancy. The current UK infant mortality rate is 4.2 per 1000 live births – for my 19th-century foremothers, the rate was 90. For comparison, that's about the same as the Central African Republic today. The painful death of so many infants was not the only cost of large families. Serious overcrowding in substandard and damp housing, the spread of terrible disease, hunger and inadequate diet, lack of affordable healthcare all affected the poorest and largest families most. Poor health throughout life meant lower life expectancy, educational opportunities were lessened, children had to take on adult responsibilities of childcare and work at a shockingly early age, and the pressure on familial relationships was intense.

Women gave birth so often because they couldn't not. They had no alternative; what contraception existed was by no means easily available. Spacing families through abstinence from sexual intercourse

required a cooperation from husbands which was culturally completely unacceptable. Marital sex was entirely under the control of
men in this intensely patriarchal society; it was a woman's duty to
obey her husband's wishes and fulfil his needs; her wishes, needs,
or indeed health, had no value – even if, like Marion Farquhar, more
than half your life between the ages of 30 and 46 were spent in a
state of pregnancy, and the rest presumably nursing babies. Religion,
culture and the law all saw women as effectively the property of their
husbands; so, a man could not rape his wife because her consent
was assumed, and if a woman was raped by another man, the offence
was primarily seen as against her husband. The Victorian idealisa-
tion, and indeed fetishisation of motherhood, domesticity and separate spheres, driven as they were by essentially economic interests,
all reinforced the view that it was a woman's lot, and place, to bear
children, and the only limit on that would be one of her fertility (the
man's fertility was never questioned).

If this was the situation for married women, it was far worse for
single women. Women were meant to be married, it was their vocation, and if they were not married (and about a third of women
never married in 19th-century Scotland), then their options were
supposed to be to go into service or factories if they were working
class, or become spinster daughters and maiden aunts if they were
middle class. Above all, they were never, never, never to have sex!
The penalties for women who did, and who were seen to have done
so by becoming pregnant, were brutal, and ran from loss of reputation, exclusion from the family and home and loss of livelihood, to
poverty, prostitution, destitution and death. Not surprisingly, these
penalties did not apply to the men, the fiction being maintained that
pregnancy was entirely the woman's fault and the woman's responsibility. The worst that was likely to happen to the men was that
they would be hastened into marriage, as at least one of my great-
great-grandfathers was.

The other alternatives were too awful to contemplate (though desperate women did, of course). In the minutes of the Kirk Session of the parish church in Kirkoswald in the 19th century, alongside the lists of new communicants and the raising of a fund by subscription from the elders in order to reduce the price of oatmeal for poor householders within the parish, is a story which emphasises the plight of women giving unsanctioned birth. From 1812, it describes a Session meeting enquiring into the circumstances of how a female newborn child was left at the door of one James Campbell, innkeeper in Kirkoswald. The Session *'had made enquiry through the parishes … and Girvan but could not find out the unatural mother or person that had laid down the child'*.[4]

On the night in question, hearing a knocking at the door sometime after midnight, James Campbell went down and asked who was there; no one answered, but he thought he heard someone moving away from the door and going down the road. Going upstairs, he looked out of the window: he saw a white thing at the door and at the same time heard the murmurs of a child. He called to his servant Agnes Neil to take in the child … *'he saw no other person at the time he called to his servant till she had taken up the child that he remained a few minutes at the window after the child was taken up and the reason why he did not alarm the neighbours that he was afraid that he might be murdered if he went out that upon his return to the kitchen he found his servant with the child on her knee warming its feet at the fire … further that he has not ground of suspision either who left the child at his door or the mother of it, that the child was a little sore on one cheek as if rubbed with the carrying but from the cleaness of its cloes thinks that it had not been carried far.'* Then, the Session heard, *'Margt Neilson a widow woman declared that she had examined the child and that it was a female child and appeared not to be many days old and that it was neatly swaddled up and done by a person of some experience.'*[5] The Session in the meantime appointed that the child be given to a proper nurse as soon as one could be procured and that all diligent search be made to find out the natural mother, and if not soon found that the child be baptised and the members of the Session should act as sponsors.

And from the Minute Book of the High Court of Justiciary – South Circuit in 1860, a grimmer story, detailing the indictment of Janet Bryan, an unmarried 38-year-old woman from Kilwinning in Ayrshire, for child murder. The records describe how, alone, she gave birth to twins, female and male, in a farm field, who she claimed had been born dead, and how she then buried them in a nearby shallow ditch. This testimony was then given by a policeman:

'William Hall Police Constable at Kilwinning aged 24. He had been informed by John Frew, labourer at Burrelholes that Janet Bryan was suspected of giving birth to a child in a field in Dykeneuk Farm. He went to the place and searched, but found no sign of the child. Next day, he went to Burrelholes, but Janet Bryan denied having given birth to a child or concealing it. He ordered her to be examined by a doctor and it was then she admitted giving birth to a child. He took her into custody and on the way to Kilwinning, she admitted that she had given birth to twins – a boy and a girl. She agreed to show him where she had buried them. She said they were dead when they were born. At the roadside on the farm of Goldcraig occupied by James Heggie, they went through a gate into the plantation. She took him to a small ditch and there covered with grass he found the children, lying on their backs one next to the other. They were lying in water. She said 'godsake not to lift them till it was dark'. He then took her to Kilwining and returned with a box and lifted the children and washed them in a small burn. The children were handed to Drs Haldane and Montgomerie for post mortems. Janet Bryan told him that she had planned to take them to a lodging house in Kilwinning and get them buried, but that she did not have enough money. He noticed a teaspoon of earth in the mouths of both children. It was not the same earth as that in which they had been found. It was dark brown, whereas the earth in the ditch was yellowish clay. He had removed the earth from their mouths' [6]

There followed evidence from at least five people who had seen Janet come or go from the field, and from others who testified that they had not known that she was 'in the family way'. Janet herself made a declaration:

'On the Friday at midday, she had given birth to two children, a male and female. The female had been born first, but did not breathe. About 20 minutes to ½ an hour later, the boy was born. He breathed. She rolled him up in a cloth, but he did not breathe again. Neither cried. She planned to go to Kilwinning to bury them, but felt weak and the children were heavy and so she put them in a drain and covered them with dry soil. There had been no water in the drain. She denied drowning them or inflicting any violence on them. She then went to her cousin, Elizabeth Milligan and borrowed 2/- from her and went to Kilwinning Station and took the train to Troon and went to see her uncle. William Milligan at Loans. She stayed there till the Monday. Then the police had come and she had taken them to the drain. She had not told anyone she was pregnant.'[7]

The doctors found that she had given birth. There followed a fairly detailed post-mortem report, but they found no evidence of violence to the children. Janet Bryan pleaded guilty to child murder, and was sentenced to ten years' penal servitude.

***

When I look back on these foremothers of the 19th century, I see that all of the legal and cultural restrictions which have made me into a feminist activist in my own life deeply affected them also, and that many of these constraints actually originated during their lifetimes. Agnes Hamilton and her daughters were successful businesswomen in spite of the considerable discrimination that faced women in their trading city, and used their money to support and defend the other women in their family. Catherine Lyall, a rich woman in her own right before her marriage, saw her wealth become the legal property of her husband. Her large house, small family and foreign travel did not guarantee Catherine Lyall a happy life or a peaceful end. Ann Miller had to go into domestic service when she was nearly sixty to help her bankrupt husband pay off his creditors. Janet Aitken, the cotton handloom weaver, and Mary Wilson both had large families in the hard conditions of the Industrial Revolution, moving often and raising sons who went down the mines and daughters who went into domestic service. Marrion Gilchrist, the island schoolmaster's daughter, and Elizabeth Aitken, the ploughman's wife, both lived in insecurity and died painfully. And Marion Campbell spent most of her adult life pregnant.

Almost all of these women had lives characterised by what seems to me today as enormously hard work in challenging circumstances. The children of half of them lived in step-families. And all of them, including the middle-class families, lived in households which included lodgers and numerous extended family members. Not one of them reflected the nuclear family model which was to be held up as normative for 150 years by state, culture and church.

Notes:

1. From 'An auld friend wi' a new face', by Joanna Picken, in *Radical Renfrew: Poetry in the West of Scotland from the French Revolution to the First World War*, ed. Tom Leonard, Polygon, 1990

2. From 'A bill to prohibit the employment of women and girls in mines and collieries, to regulate the employment of boys, and make provisions for the safety of persons working therein. 22 June 1842'

3. App. 258 Lord Robert Grosvenor. Sig. 227 – The Petition of the Coalminers employed at Thankerton, Middle Ward of Lanarkshire

4. From Kirkoswald Kirk Session Records:
    www.maybole.org/community/kirkoswald/
    kirkoswaldkirksessionrecords.htm

5. ibid. 4

6. ibid. 4

7. ibid. 4

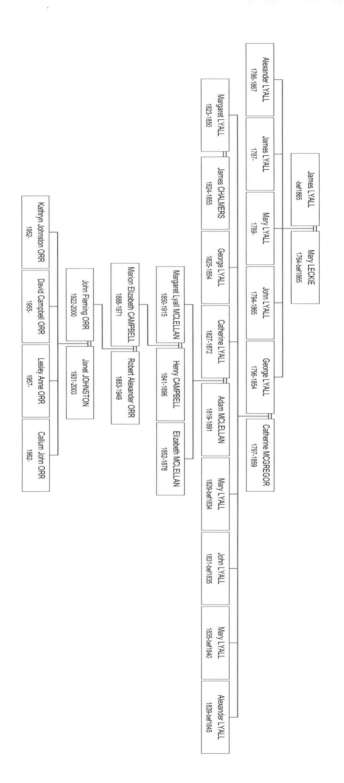

Alexander LYALL
1786-1867

James LYALL
1787-

Mary LYALL
1789-

John LYALL
1794-1865

George LYALL
1796-1854

James LYALL
-bef1865

Mary LECKIE
1764-bef1865

Margaret LYALL
1823-1850

James CHALMERS
1824-1855

George LYALL
1825-1854

Catherine LYALL
1827-1872

Catherine MCGREGOR
1797-1859

Mary LYALL
1829-bef1834

John LYALL
1831-bef1835

Mary LYALL
1835-bef1840

Alexander LYALL
1839-bef1845

Margaret Lyall MCLELLAN
1850-1915

Henry CAMPBELL
1841-1896

Adam MCLELLAN
1819-1891

Elizabeth MCLELLAN
1852-1878

Marion Elizabeth CAMPBELL
1888-1971

Robert Alexander ORR
1883-1949

John Fleming ORR
1922-2000

Janet JOHNSTON
1931-2003

Kathryn Johnston ORR
1952-

David Campbell ORR
1955-

Lesley Anne ORR
1957-

Callum John ORR
1962-

A mid-Victorian family, 1822-1891

The radical weavers

In tracing our forebears back over 350 years, my siblings and I were unsurprised to discover that the great majority of them lived lives characterised by poverty, insecurity and illness well into the 20th century. They were ordinary Scots, and that was the experience of most people in Scotland for most of that time. Therefore, it was intriguing to find two who were in fact extremely rich, both by the standards of their day and by present-day calculation: our great-great-great-grandfather, George Lyall, and his daughter, our great-great-grandmother, Catherine Lyall McLellan.

George Lyall was born in 1796 in Paisley the youngest of five children of James Lyall, a weaver, and his wife Mary Leckie, a weaver's daughter. Paisley was a town built on fine weaving, both linen and especially silk, and the successful introduction of silk gauze weaving in 1759 brought great prosperity to the town. In 1805, the weaving of Paisley shawls was introduced, eventually becoming the main product of the town, and in 1834, over a million pounds' worth of shawls were produced locally. At least two of George's brothers were also weavers, one of them a gauze weaver.

But, like many industries in the rapidly developing capitalist economy of 19th-century Scotland, weaving was also subject to intermittent periods of market fluctuation, unemployment and wage insecurity, in a time when the lack of any but the most rudimentary and harsh 'poor relief' brought great hardship to many. In 1812, a court action by the weavers' union to have agreed wage rates established by law, in order to prevent employers driving them ever downwards, was successful in the Court of Session – but there was no compulsion attached to the judgement, which was then simply ignored by the manufacturers. The weavers went on strike, and 40,000 weavers across Scotland joined the strike. But there was no strike pay or poor relief available, and striking itself had been made illegal by the Combination Acts of 1799 and 1800. Strike committee members were jailed, the strikers were intimidated by strikebreakers, and the strike collapsed after 12 weeks. The weavers were starved back to work at the old rates.

William Finlayson, the secretary to the weavers' union, wrote a bitter poem entitled: 'Weavers' Lament: On the Failure of the Celebrated Strike of Weaving, for a Minimum of Wages, in 1812'. Its first four verses make the grim situation of the weavers painfully evident:

Ye Weavers cease to mourn an' grieve,
Can bitter sighs your case relieve?
Nae mair let hope your hearts deceive,
> *Fix'd is your fate;*
Be thankfu' ye're allow'd to weave
> *At ony rate.*

Deaf to your earnest cries, an' pray'rs,
Against you ilka door declares,
Nor King, nor Parliamentar cares,
> *Nor local pow'rs,*
A' busy wi' their ain affairs,
> *They mind not ours.*

For refuge whither can we fly?
What ither schemes of succour try?
Where'er we sen' the sorrowing eye,
> *Or turn the head,*
Wives, weans, an' aged parents die,
> *For lack o' bread.*

Alas! That any 'ministration
Should glory to involve a nation,
In ruin, honour, an' starvation,
> *An' even disdain*
To make the slightest reparation,
> *Tho' it complain ...*[1]

The weavers of Paisley were said to be the most intelligent, the most widely read and the most radical of all Scottish workers. Highly skilled, they were at the heart of the radicalism running through the town – a hotbed of early trades unionism – which placed it at the centre of the Radical War of 1820. The Radical War of 1820 was a popular insurrection of thousands of West of Scotland workers, which took place during a week of strikes and unrest across central Scotland. Demands for radical reform in Britain and Ireland had gained force during the French Revolution, but had then been stifled during the war against Napoleon.

Economic downturn after the wars ended brought increasing unemployment, destitution and unrest across the industrial parts of Britain. The Peterloo Massacre of 1819 in Manchester, when a peaceful public meeting of around 60,000 people was charged at by the Yeomanry, resulting in 18 deaths and 400 injured, sparked huge protests in Scotland. Skilled workers, particularly weavers, sought action to reform, or even to replace, an uncaring London government with a provisional Scottish one. The landed classes, terrified that this was importing the revolutionary zeal of France into Scotland, which might have a similar drastic outcome for them, raised militia, and the government enlisted a network of spies and informers to entice law-breaking in order to stamp out the movement, which they did with effective brutality.

And a later economic depression in 1842 brought this comment from the Provost of Paisley: '*Unemployment was the rule … few workmen of Paisley were employed: they were broken up and found to be wandering about in every town in the country, begging for bread, independent of those thousands whom they had at home supported by charity*'.[2]

The Paisley vintner

In spite of the ferment of political activity taking place in his home town, and possibly in his own family, there is no record of George Lyall being a Radical. Nor did he become rich through weaving; in fact, it is hard for us to understand quite how he became so rich. He established himself as a wine and spirit merchant, with a shop in the town centre, and certainly there is always a market for alcohol. But this was an industrial town, ravaged by periods of mass unemployment and poverty. Nor was he providing a niche service. In this town of 60,000 people, there were literally hundreds of spirit dealers. Perhaps the fact that he was also a wine merchant offered him a different class of customer. And in fact, the first half of the 19th century saw unparalleled levels of alcohol consumption across every class and profession. Permissive legislation, low duty and not least, the lack of clean water in many places led to a situation in which alcohol played a central role in the daily lives and socialising of every class. Though there is a tendency today to be somewhat mocking of the temperance movement which emerged in response to the uses and abuses of alcohol, these abuses were indeed very great: they often led to addiction, debt, impoverishment, family breakdown and domestic violence.

However he managed to be so successful, by the middle of the 19th century, George Lyall was very prosperous indeed, with two premises in Paisley and another in Glasgow, moving from a tenement flat in Moss Street to a nine-roomed house, Abbotsburn (described as *a neat dwelling house with gardens attached*), and taking seaside holidays with his family at Seamill on the Ayrshire coast.

He had married Catherine McGregor, herself a weaver's daughter, in 1822, and together they had seven children between 1823 and 1839. But their family life had been marked by loss. The four youngest children died in childhood. The oldest child, Margaret,

George Lyall and Adam McLellan, 1854

married James Chalmers, the son of a bleacher (a process in the textile industry). George had taken his son-in-law into the family business, as manager of one of his shops. George Junior was also working for his father. And Catherine, the third child, our great-great-grandmother, born in 1827, had in 1850 married Adam McLellan, a Glasgow clothier, hatter and merchant eight years her senior. In the 1851 census, they are recorded as living in Oswald Street in Glasgow, with a servant, and as a visitor, Catherine's mother Catherine, perhaps there to assist with her three-month-old granddaughter, Margaret. A second daughter, Elizabeth, was born the following year.

But the life of the Lyall family continued to be marked by tragedy. In July 1850, Margaret Chalmers died aged 27. On the 15th July 1854, George Senior made a will. He was 58 years old, but presumably knew that his death was imminent; he died four days later. The will was drawn up by the clerk to a Paisley Writer (solicitor), John Dunn, and in the presence of his wife Catherine, and witnessed by a Glasgow spirit merchant, and by his resident gardener. In it, he named his son George, his son-in-law James Chalmers (then working as his clerk), his other son-in-law Adam McLellan, and the Writer John Dunn, as his trustees and executors.

The will is very long, ten pages, and it is very complicated. George Senior instructs his executors to pay any debts, his funeral expenses and any costs of the executors from his estate. He leaves an annuity of £100 to his wife Catherine McGregor, as well as *'the free use and enjoyment during her lifetime of the mansion house garden and grounds of Abbotsburn with the whole furniture and plenishing thereof'*; this would leave her very comfortably off. He leaves James Chalmers a legacy of £500. He leaves his granddaughters Margaret and Elizabeth, then aged 3 and 2, £400 and £300 respectively. He leaves his remaining siblings, the weavers Alexander and John, and his sister Mary, a weekly allowance of seven shillings to be paid for the rest of their lives. They were all in their sixties by this time, so this really constituted an old-age pension for all of them, presumably paid weekly in cash because they had no bank accounts.

Having provided generously for his whole family, George then bequeaths Abbotsburn, with all its grounds and contents, to his son George, with entry after his mother's death. He leaves the rest of his estate to be equally divided between George Junior and Catherine McLellan or her lawful daughters. He notes that a large part of the estate will consist of his trading business as a wine and spirit merchant in Paisley and Glasgow, along with all the debts owed to him through the business. He states his intention that George Junior should succeed him as owner of the business, and instructs his executors to arrange for a full valuation of the business to be carried out by a trusted person, including the Paisley premises, the spirit cellar, the stock held in Paisley and Glasgow and all the debts owed to him. An extensive list of debtors is appended to the will.

He furthermore authorises his trustees to allow his son to obtain a loan of up to £3000 over and above his own half share of the inheritance, to be repaid with interest to the estate within five years. He empowers his trustees to act as *'tutors and curators'* for his grandchildren before their majority, gives them power of sale or investment with regard to the estate, to add to the number of trustees as and when they think it necessary, and to act in all matters as they see fit.

And in a striking demonstration of the power of a patriarch to impose his will from beyond the grave, another condition is made: *'And further I do hereby provide and declare that in case any of my said children shall repudiate this settlement and claim their legal provisions, or shall by any means prevent this settlement from taking effect, then such child shall forfeit all right to such share of my estate and effects as I may freely dispose of by law, which in such event shall access and belong to the child abiding by this testament.'* This sends a clear message to George Junior that his inheritance is conditional on continuing in the family business – or is this a message to Catherine for some undisclosed reason?

In the event, it was all academic. Before the end of 1854, George Junior was also dead, suddenly and rather horribly after being bitten by a rabid dog. The complications this further disaster caused soon became evident. The document which contains the text of George Lyall Senior's will of 1854 is dated 12th April 1855, and is titled Trust Disposition and Settlement of George Lyall. In it, James Chalmers testifies that Adam McLellan and John Dunn are now acting as executors not just for George Senior but also for George Junior, who has died intestate (that is, without making a will, which is not so surprising, given that he was only 29 at the time of his unexpected death). They have completed the inventory of the estate, and report that its value is just over £13,000. It doesn't sound so much today, but in 1855, it was the equivalent of being comfortably in the millionaire range.

The final settlement of this estate comes in a document dated 2nd June 1859. It is the inventory of George Junior's estate (basically his share of the inheritance), and all of it, £4115, goes to his next of kin, his sister Catherine Lyall McLellan. Added to her own share, Catherine's inheritance in total comprised Abbotsburn, its grounds and contents, the business and all its assets, and the equivalent of over £8 million in money and shares. By the standards of her own era (and indeed, by the standards of today) Catherine, aged 28, was now a seriously wealthy woman.

The man of property

Or rather, since this was before the Married Women's Property (Scotland) Act of 1881, Adam McLellan was now a seriously wealthy man. Before 1881, when a woman married, she lost all her own property and rights of inheritance, and any such would immediately become the possession of her husband. Whether she owned it, earned it or inherited it, it now belonged to him. Effectively, her personhood was absorbed into his, and she ceased to exist independently in any legal sense. Nor did she retain any control over her property; though legally still the owner by dint of her absorption into her husband, she could make no decisions about it, or object to any her husband made, or draw on it without his permission. She, and any children, were absolutely dependent on him.

This was certainly true of Catherine. Still a young woman, all her six siblings and her father were dead, her brother-in-law James Chalmers had died in 1855, and her mother died in August 1859. Catherine and her girls had no one except Adam, and he controlled all her wealth.

Having already spent their honeymoon in Paris, the McLellans marked their newfound prosperity by taking a trip to the Paris Exhibition (or Exposition Universelle) of 1855, a great trade fair, industrial and agricultural showcase, and fine art exhibition. Its display of the

Adam McLellan and Catherine Lyall McLellan on their honeymoon, 1850

finest Bordeaux wines (which led to the introduction of the Bordeaux Wine Official Classification) may well have been of interest to the wine merchant's daughter. The photographic portraits which were taken at this time show a couple dressed in the height of mid-19th-century fashion, and though photographic styles are very much of their time, it is hard to say that they looked very cheerful.

This is also the last time that Catherine and Adam appear together in any family or official documents, or any photographs. They moved into Abbotsburn with Catherine's mother, and Adam seems to have enthusiastically embraced the role of leading businessman/man-about-town.

Over the next ten years, until 1865, Adam engaged in multiple property transactions, both as owner and as tenant. Catherine had inherited a number of properties as part of the Lyall inheritance. A tenement in New Sneddon Street, Paisley, for which Adam is recorded as the proprietor, had five tenants living in separate flats. He also owned a stable and a spirit cellar, and held the tenancy of a shop in Gilmour Street. Around this time, the Lyall wine and spirit business was sold, and presumably the flats in New Sneddon Street also.

Adam is variously described as a clothier, a tailor and a hatter, though prior to his marriage to Catherine, it is debatable how successful he was; his business had been sequestered in 1848 and he had been declared bankrupt. However, in 1855, he rented shop premises and a workshop in Queen Street, Glasgow, right in the city centre. He also rented a flat in the East End of Glasgow for one of his sisters, Catherine McKinnon.

It was around this time in 1855, that he began the family relationship with Kilcreggan, which was to last for nearly seventy years. Kilcreggan is a beautiful village on the Rosneath Peninsula on the north shore of the Firth of Clyde, about 25 miles west of Glasgow. In 1848, the Duke of Argyll, who owned the land, had feued the south and west coasts of the Rosneath Peninsula to property developers, and had built steamer piers to encourage building. Kilcreggan and its neighbouring village of Cove became *the* fashionable place for wealthy Glasgow merchants and shipowners to build summer homes or even full-time residences. The Duke's chamberlains retained a tight control over the feued properties to ensure that high building standards were maintained, and the large plots and high costs of building and maintaining properties designed by leading Scottish architects meant that these houses were only for the seriously well-off.

Adam was one of the merchants who commissioned the construction of a new house. Between 1855 and 1857, he rented several villas in Kilcreggan, including Seaview, in which he installed his other sister, Elizabeth McLellan. Was he renting these houses for summer holidays and weekends? Was he looking for a suitable plot to build on, or waiting for the final settlement of his wife's inheritance? In the event, in May 1860, Adam feued a plot of land on Argyll Road from Alexander Leckie (who had himself feued it from the Duke of Argyll). The house he built there, originally called Park Place, renamed Albert Park on the death of Prince Albert in 1861, eventually became the family home of his daughter Margaret and her husband, Henry Campbell.

Adam's investment in land and property did not end there. By 1865, he had taken on the tenancy of two neighbouring farms near Maybole in Ayrshire, Knockdon and Otterden Mains, though whether he did any actual farming is not clear, and seems unlikely, given his complete lack of farming experience or background, and his many other activities – because Adam was also becoming something of a public figure.

The public man

In 1857, he took a leading role in the by-election campaign of Humphrey Crum-Ewing, a Whig politician who was a member of a well-to-do local family. The by-election had been caused by the death of the sitting MP, Archibald Hastie, a Radical politician who had held the seat for over 20 years. The only other candidate was another Radical, William Taylor Haly. Crum-Ewing had a very distinctive *curriculum vitae*. He was the owner of large plantations in British Guyana, chairman of the Glasgow West India Association and a director of the Colonial Company of London. All of these identified him as a man whose wealth had deep roots in slavery.

The Glasgow West India Association had been founded in 1807 by Crum-Ewing's uncle, James Ewing, a few months after the legislation to abolish the British Atlantic slave trade had been passed. Its primary and stated purpose was to protect the interests of the tobacco and sugar trades, on which the economy of Glasgow and the West of Scotland had become so dependent. Over the following thirty years, it became the most powerful group representing slaving interests outside London.

It presented itself initially as a benevolent organisation concerned with the well-being of enslaved people, it claimed that reports describing the horrendous conditions and abuses prevalent in the West Indies were 'fake news', and it campaigned relentlessly against the various groups involved in the movement for the abolition of chattel slavery. As the tide of public opinion turned against them, it sought at every point to delay the emancipation of enslaved people, and promoted the introduction of the 'Apprenticeship Scheme', essentially bondage under another name. In the end, the colonial planters and their supporters in the UK had to accept defeat and abolition of slavery, but not before they had secured compensation which *'represented over thirteen times the collective profits of sugar, rum and coffee on West Indian property'*.[3]

It was dispiriting, to say the least, to discover that, only twenty years after the abolition of slavery, our great-great-grandfather had been campaigning for someone with such a background; especially given the consistent and widespread support that Paisley had given to both the movement to end the Atlantic slave trade and the movement for complete abolition. But this probably says as much about the state of the franchise in the UK in 1857 as it does about Scotland's role in slavery, about which then, and more or less ever since, Scots have had an almost total, and convenient, memory lapse. Certainly, the sitting MP whose demise had brought about the by-election, though in name a Radical, had twice voted against emancipation.

There is a long, detailed and highly entertaining account in the *Paisley Herald* of 12th December 1857 of the events of the by-election. It begins with an account of the meeting for nomination: '... *the nomination of candidates took place in front of the County Buildings, Paisley. There might be about five or six thousand persons present, a mere tithe of whom were electors.*'[4] (At this time, only about 13% of adult men, and no women, were eligible to vote, and this *after* the first major Reform Act.) There then follows a description which makes contemporary elections, even the most contentious, seem tame in comparison, fully punctuated by the insertion of sound effects – cheers, catcalls, groans, hisses, boos and jeers – into the text of the article.

One of the candidates, Crum-Ewing, was not actually present, apparently travelling in Europe for some mysterious and much-mocked reason, and was represented by his son. The other was a lawyer on the third of five unsuccessful attempts to enter Parliament, mostly for his home town of Poole in Dorset. The proposers of the candidates, one of whom was Adam McLellan, who was thoroughly jeered by the crowd, then gave lengthy speeches, which were almost completely free of any matters of policy or political import, but were devoted to outlining a long list of outrages and calumnies on the part of each other's opponents. These ranged from false representation and deceit, bribery and corruption to the undue influence of the Kirk and the fiddling of expenses. The matter was complicated by the fact that the supporters of each candidate seemed to have changed sides several times.

The Sheriff overseeing the proceedings then took a popular vote of all present by a show of hands, which Mr Haly (who seems from other accounts of him to have been a genuine Radical) was deemed to have won by a large margin. This popular acclamation was not, however, reflected in the actual poll, which returned Mr Crum-Ewing to the House of Commons by 767 votes to 98 votes. It was also reported that *'after the result of the poll was known, a party of juveniles and others commenced to throw stones and other missiles. The police force succeeded in restoring order, but in case of a riot, the Pensioners were mustered in the Barracks'.*[5] Aside from the irrepressible image this last sentence suggests to the 21st-century reader, the whole story is a vivid reflection of the dismal and truncated nature of democracy in mid-Victorian Scotland, particularly the West of Scotland, whereby a middle-class electorate of Whig/Liberal property-owning men were able to return politicians who represented their own interests and ideologies, without paying much heed at all to working-class voices.

Adam continued on his upwardly mobile path, enabled by his wife's money. He became a Freemason. In January 1860, the *Glasgow Daily Herald* carried a report of the 52nd Annual Dinner, held in the George Hotel Glasgow, of the Thistle and Rose Society, one of the numerous Friendly Societies of mutual association for the purposes of insurance, pensions, saving and cooperative banking which were formed in the 19th century. In his remarks, the Chairman congratulated the Society on having paid out well below the average level in sickness benefits, this being attributable to the fact '*the class of which this society is composed is more select than the average*'.[6] He then proposed a toast to the prosperity of the Thistle and Rose Society and its benefits for future generations.

The next toast proposed was to the Lord Provost, Magistrates and Council of Glasgow, coupled with the name of Mr Adam McLellan. Mr McLellan, in replying, said that when meetings like the present honoured the gentlemen conducting the public business of this large city, it must at all times be to them a pleasing recompense – a recompense next to that of a satisfied mind. He could assure them that the labours of the Town Council were very numerous and arduous, and outlined these labours. After a couple of witty and well-received remarks, he then proposed a toast to the Evangelical Clergy of Scotland, one of whose number duly replied, complimenting the Society on having become quite an institution of mark in Glasgow. A dozen more toasts were proposed and drunk, no doubt justifying the reporter's conclusion that the evening was most agreeably spent.

In February 1862, Adam McLellan Esq. of Abbotsburn chaired the second Annual Festival of Glasgow Natives of Paisley, held in the City Hall. In his chairman's remarks, which were fully reported by the *Paisley Herald*, he commended the importance of friendship in trade. He reminded his audience of famous sons of Paisley, including Alexander Wilson, weaver, poet and ornithologist (who had actually fled to the United States of America, having been imprisoned for his radical views); John Wilson, the Tory Professor of Moral Philosophy at Glasgow University; Robert Tannahill, weaver and poet; a man named Henning, who had apparently played an important part in the early restoration of the Elgin Marbles (generally now agreed to have caused irreparable damage); and Lord Clyde, the British Army general who put down the Indian Mutiny. He touched on the founding of Paisley in 1488, and on the improving impact of the Reformation. He then offered a short history of the textile industry in the town, its founding by a woman, and its present-day flourishing. Truly, it was a comprehensive address on the subject of Paisley.[7]

A fractured family

Adam was by now a well-regarded member of the West of Scotland mercantile classes, and a confident public speaker. His family life is rather more obscure, however, and clearly became unhappy. The 1861 census shows them in three different places. Adam, described as a tailor, is listed as a visitor in a hotel in Pannal, a village just outside Harrogate. Catherine is listed at a private house in Liverpool. And ten-year-old Maggie (as she was now known) and eight-year-old Elizabeth were in Abbotsburn, with a servant and a visitor called Minnie McGregor, aged 29. She may have been a relative from their maternal grandmother's family. Catherine McGregor Lyall herself had died two years before.

Studio photographs from a Paisley photographer's around this time show Maggie, aged about ten and twelve, formally posed in the somewhat cumbersome clothes of her day, complete with pantaloons, and holding her flowered boater. Like most photos of this era, she looks very serious.

The next few years were very difficult for the members of the McLellan family. In October 1865, Catherine was admitted as a private patient to the Crichton Royal Institution in Dumfries, a charitable hospital for people who were mentally ill, and who had the means (and the rates were considerable) to pay for treatment in a handsome building laid out in 40 acres of grounds, including pleasure gardens, with private rooms and a good staff-to-patients ratio. (The paupers in the Southern Counties Asylum nearby, on the contrary, sleep sixteen to a dormitory.) An 1857 Royal Commission Report describes the facilities:

> 'There are abundant means of recreation and amusement. An omnibus and other carriages are provided, which enable the patients to make frequent excursions; and there is a small theatre, seated for 110 persons, in which concerts are given, and plays performed. The attendants are principally the performers, but Dr Browne takes care that at least one patient shall be among the actors to keep up an interest in the performances. Writing and drawing materials, and books, are liberally supplied, and courses of lectures also are delivered. During the ensuing summer a triple course is contemplated, on botany, chemistry, and natural history, by Dr Browne and his assistants. There is a library of 5000 volumes, and an extensive museum of natural history, the specimens of which serve for illustrating the lectures. Dr Browne lately gave a course of twenty-five lectures to his assistants and the attendants, on their duties, and on the nature and management of mental disease.

> 'The concerts and other amusements are attended by patients from both houses. There is a billiard-room, and during the summer a house is taken at the sea-side, for the benefit of the patients.'[8]

Catherine was admitted from Knockdon Farm in Maybole; although the Crichton Institution was supposedly for patients from the counties of Dumfries, Wigtown and Kirkcudbright, and Maybole is in Ayrshire, it's possible that this was more discreet than admission to an asylum in Ayr, only a few miles away. She was discharged in February 1866, into the care of her husband (described as a farmer) and returned to Maybole. Hospital records note that her condition on discharge was *'recovered'*.

However, her respite was to be brief. On 16th May, just three months later, Catherine Lyall McLellan, aged 38 years old, of Knockdon Farm, Maybole, was admitted to the Glasgow Royal Asylum for Lunatics at Gartnavel. She was recorded as a farmer's wife, and her religious persuasion as United Presbyterian Church. The length of time of her insanity was given as around one year, and this was stated as her second attack. The supposed cause of the attack was said to be *'domestic reverses'*. The examining doctor describes her as being of vacant appearance, with a childish demeanour, insolent and incoherent. She claims that she is full of electricity, and is to be blown up. The signatory to her admission, noted as her next of kin, was her 15-year-old daughter Maggie. But this time, her hospitalisation was not voluntary; she was being committed.

The circumstances surrounding Catherine's third hospitalisation are truly shocking. On December 10th, 1867, she was once again admitted to Gartnavel Asylum. But this time, on the admission papers, she is described as a pauper, at present in Govan Poorhouse. Her previous address is given as Downie Terrace, an address which does not exist in Glasgow (though there is a Doune Terrace in the West End), and her next of kin as Janie McLellan, daughter, also residing in Downie Terrace. There is no record in our family of this person, and it is not either of her daughters. The papers state that she is a danger to herself and to others. The GP who had examined her in Govan Poorhouse reports that she is of unsound mind on the following grounds: *'she is incoherent and violent, excited and dangerous to herself, filthy in her actions and very obscene in her talk. The nurse states that she has destructive tendencies and requires constant watching.'* A second doctor confirms this, adding that she sings, laughs and talks to herself, uses violence to the other patients and also tried to stick a pin into her throat.[9]

Poor Catherine! We can only assume that in her deranged state, she was found wandering in the streets of Glasgow, and was either taken, or found her way to, the Poorhouse, which was then located in Eglinton Street, in the Gorbals district on the south side of the river, quite near to the city centre. Clearly very ill and confused, it's hard to understand what she was doing in Glasgow, and why she was alone and apparently penniless. Where were her family? It seems that around this time, Adam, and perhaps the girls, were living in Kilcreggan, though a studio portrait of Maggie, now a beautiful young woman of seventeen, had been taken at a studio in Ayr in the September of 1867, so it's possible that she was still living in Maybole. In any event, presumably Catherine's family was traced, and she was discharged from Gartnavel in July 1868, recorded as 'well'.

In 1870, when she was 43 years old, Catherine made a will, in which she named her two daughters, who were then still only 20 and 18, as her executors, and in which she bequeathed her estate to them, omitting any mention of her husband. And in 1871, the census shows her once again at her own family home, Abbotsburn in Paisley, where she is described as household head, aged 43, wife of Adam McLellan. The only other name given is that of a visitor, Eleanor McAndrew, aged 7, from Glasgow. On the same day, Adam is staying with his sister Elizabeth in the lodging house she runs in Glasgow. He is now described as a Commission Merchant (effectively a broker or middle man). Elizabeth is at Albert Park in Kilcreggan with a 17-year-old friend and a servant, and Maggie, who gives her occupation as milliner, is visiting another friend in Kilcreggan.

On 3rd April 1872, Maggie got married. She was 21 years old, and her new husband was a local farmer, ten years older, Henry Campbell. Henry was one of the sons of the enormous family of John Campbell and Marion Farquhar, born at Knockjarder Farm, Dalrymple, but now farming High Pinmore Farm near Maybole. We

Margaret McLellan in 1867 and Henry Campbell in the uniform of the Ayrshire Yeomanry in 1860

assume they met when Adam was farming at Knockdon. We don't know too much about Henry, except that he was a very successful member of the Ayrshire Yeomanry, one of the volunteer reserve forces established at the end of the 18th century to defend against the threat of revolution or invasion. First raised by the Earl of Cassilis (later the Marquis of Ailsa, Henry's landlord) their earlier years were mostly spent as an aid to the civil authorities in controlling riots across Ayrshire and beyond, most notably in Paisley. Today they are part of the Territorial Army.

On 30th May 1872, just two months after Maggie's wedding, Catherine was admitted as a private patient from Cove (Kilcreggan) to Glengall Asylum in Ayr, the district mental hospital. She was recorded as being in good physical health; her mental disorder was given as climacteric insanity (maniacal). The cause of this was said to be unknown; the episode of the mania was two days in length and she had had one previous episode five years before. Her elder daughter, Margaret McLellan Campbell, of High Pinmore, was listed as the contact.

Her casebook notes stated her to be suicidal, but no members of her family were known to have been insane. Her medical notes state that she had delusions as to arrangements in her son-in-law's house regarding appliances for electrical purposes, delusions as to having had messages from heaven, and excitement and restlessness of manner. Delusions concerning electrical appliances around the walls of the room in her son-in-law's house continued, as did those of having had personal intercourse with the almighty as to her own fate and that of others. Also written in her case notes were the following recommendations:

'Yew trees (don't let her eat)
Don't restrain without permission
Record all accidents within one day
Ensure area of accommodation is safe' [10]

Just over three months after her admission, she died after a week of illness; the cause of her death was given as paralysis. In her will, this woman who had inherited a fortune, left just £175.

But what was really wrong with Catherine? The term climacteric insanity (maniacal as opposed to melancholic) is not a recognised diagnosis today. What it actually refers to is the menopause, and the tendency of the Victorian male medical profession to pathologise the natural stages and cycles of female reproduction. So, insanity was believed to be one possible symptom of menopause. Today, it's possible that she would be diagnosed with bipolar disorder, or even schizophrenia, perhaps triggered by the extraordinary personal loss of her parents and all six of her siblings. She would be treated with a combination of medicine and therapy, and enabled to maintain a good quality of life.

Her delusions concerning the electrical appliances in her son-in-law's house are interesting. In 1870, domestic electricity was at a very early stage of transmission. The farmhouse at High Pinmore could not have had electrical appliances around the walls; but popular culture tended to regard electricity as a mysterious force with strange powers which could bend the laws of nature. Nor do beliefs about having had personal messages from heaven seem particularly delusional in a century characterised by extreme religious piety. Many clergy claimed these. What seems clear today is that the contents of Catherine's delusions were shaped by her class and culture, and the age she lived in.

It is tempting to deduce a more Gothic explanation: that Catherine was committed to the asylum by an unsympathetic husband wishing to free himself of any constraints his wife may have tried to place on the spending of her fortune. Such actions were not unknown, and there is a long history, and literature, of the mad woman in the attic, of women being incarcerated on spurious grounds which, when examined, turned out to be really about economic self-interest.

Or was the explanation something even darker? Was she suffering from what used to be called general paralysis of the insane, now more commonly called general paresis. This is a now rare form of dementia from syphilis of the nervous system. It is a feature of the third (tertiary) stage of untreated syphilis, and occurs 10-20 years after infection in a small proportion of cases. The condition is characterised by personality change, loss of self-care and social inhibitions, delusions of grandeur, mania, depression, gradual impairment of judgement and concentration and sometimes delusions of persecution. It is a progressive condition, and was inevitably fatal, until the discovery of penicillin many years later made full recovery a possibility. The trajectory of Catherine's illness would accord with this diagnosis, and possibly she had been infected with syphilis by Adam in the early years of her marriage.

Whatever the truth of this sad story, the same year Adam retired at the early age of 53, his public life at an end, and made over Albert Park to Maggie and Elizabeth (who died of pulmonary oedema in 1878). He lived for the rest of his life with Maggie and Henry and their children in Kilcreggan, where he died in 1891 aged 72.

The challenges facing Maggie, who seems to have spent her entire life supporting other people, were not over yet. In the year after her marriage and the birth of her first child, a civil action was taken out against Henry to force him to acknowledge paternity of a child recently born to a farm servant at High Pinmore. In all of our family communications and conversations across three generations, none of us was aware of the existence of this half great-aunt; she was apparently a very well-kept secret. At the end of the 1870s, Henry and Maggie moved to Kilcreggan, and from 1881, Henry is described as a retired farmer (though he was only in his early forties, so presumably as a result of ill-health, or perhaps shame about the paternity suit, which had become public knowledge). In the 1891 census, he gives his occupation as 'coach proprietor', and in 1896 he died of a tuberculosis-related disease, aged fifty-five.

Maggie was left as a widow to raise and support a family of five children, aged between eight and twenty-three. Their firstborn, John, had died aged 20, also of tuberculosis. The resourceful Maggie had already been taking in boarders since 1881; quite an undertaking with several small children and a husband and father to look after as well. By 1901, Maggie had rented a large flat near Charing Cross in Glasgow, and she moved back and forwards between there and Albert Park for the rest of her life, taking lodgers in both places, and sometimes renting out Albert Park in its entirety for the summer months.

Wedding of Catherine Lyall Campbell and John Alexander Todd, Glasgow, 1900

Meanwhile, the family grew up and scattered to all corners of the British Empire: Adam to Australia; Henry to Vancouver in Canada; Margaret's husband to the Gold Coast (Ghana today); Catherine with her husband to Worthing on the south coast of England. The only one who remained in Scotland was our grandmother, Marion Elizabeth Campbell, who married a Glasgow minister.

There is a family photograph of Catherine's wedding in Glasgow in 1900, with all of the Albert Park family resplendent in their fashionable wedding clothes. They don't look poor. But the family fortune had long since dissipated: on large families, on property, perhaps on bad investments, on the costs of treating long-term illness and by Adam's drinking it away. Looking back at a mid-Victorian family, several things stand out: the profoundly and thoroughly undemocratic nature of British, and Scottish, society; the economic reliance of the West of Scotland on British imperialism, including plantation slavery; the increasingly gendered nature of society in an implacably class-divided country; and the surprisingly progressive treatment of mental illness in Scotland. And in the middle of it all, the individuals who managed to work within the constraints of their time to survive and thrive – and the ones who didn't.

Notes:

1. From 'Weaver's Lament', by William Finlayson, in *Radical Renfrew: Poetry in the West of Scotland from the French Revolution to the First World War*, ed. Tom Leonard, Polygon, 1990

2. From *Industrial Nation: Work, Culture and Society in Scotland, 1800-Present*, W W Knox: Edinburgh University Press, 1999

3. Iain Whyte, from *Scotland and the Abolition of Black Slavery, 1756-1838*, Iain Whyte, Edinburgh University Press, 2006. Used by permission of Iain Whyte

4. *Paisley Herald*, 12th December, 1857

5. ibid. 4

6. *Glasgow Daily Herald*, 13th January, 1860

7. *Paisley Herald*, 1st March, 1862

8. Register of Discharges & Removals (Asylums): www.scottishindexes.com/institutions/15.aspx

9. Petition to the Sheriff to grant order for the reception of a patient into an asylum: from hospital records for Gartnavel

10. Gartnavel records

Conscience, contention and control,
1562-1845

'When people tell me that religion and politics don't mix, I wonder which Bible they have been reading.'

(Desmond Tutu)[1]

It's not possible to enquire into what it was like to live in Scotland over the last three hundred years without recognising the huge role that religion played in the lives of ordinary people, for good or ill; this is especially true if you come from a family that produced three generations of Presbyterian ministers and theologians in the 20th century.

When I look at the numerous graves of successive farming Campbells in peaceful Dalrymple churchyard, it's hard to imagine that anything of much significance could have happened in this quiet corner of rural Ayrshire. Yet it has a long history of theological disputation, aristocratic nest-feathering and popular protest.

Just a few miles away in the parish of Kirkoswald, the Abbey of Crossraguel had been founded as a Cluniac monastery in the 13th century by the First Earl of Carrick and had been sacked in 1307 by the army of Edward 1st of England, the 'hammer of the Scots', during the First War of Scottish Independence. In the year 1562, the Abbot of Crossraguel was Quintin Kennedy, the son of the Second Earl of Cassilis, one of only five nobles who had opposed the three Acts passed in 1560 by the Scottish Reformation Parliament. These Acts had rejected the authority of the Pope, abolished the jurisdiction of the Roman Catholic Church in Scotland, ratified and adopted the Scots Confession of Faith and declared celebration of the Mass to be a punishable offence – ultimately, for repeat offenders, by death.

The Abbot was clearly a man of considerable piety and learning, and an ardent defender of his church. The Statistical Accounts of Scotland 1791-1845, in the entry for Maybole, which was written by the local Church of Scotland minister, Rev. George Gray, described him, somewhat ambiguously, as *'one of the most learned, upright and liberal of the servants of Popery'*.[2] As passions were raised and argument raged across the country about this unparalleled and undemocratic set of decisions (whatever the popular feeling, Parliament actually at that point consisted of less than 200 unelected nobles, lairds and church dignitaries), Quintin Kennedy preached a sermon in the Parish Church of Kirkoswald attacking the doctrines of the Reformers and defending the traditional teaching on Communion. Learning of this, John Knox, who was visiting nearby (courting his very young second wife), arrived at Kirkoswald Church the following Sunday with a large number of supporters, hoping to engage the Abbot in dispute, but the Abbot was not there. However, hearing of Knox's visit, he wrote him a letter effectively challenging the Reformer to a theological duel on the doctrine of the sacrament of Communion, promising him safety from any injury or molestation, looking instead for *'familiar, formal and gentle reasoning'*.[3] Knox accepted the challenge, and so took place 'The Great Debate at Maybole'.

The participants met on 28th September 1562 at 8am in the house of the Provost of Maybole. It must have been a big house, because as well as the main protagonists, each had with him forty supporters; there were minute-takers and various members of the nobility and gentry of the county, all in the presence of the Abbot's uncle, the Third Earl of Cassilis. They disagreed over the prayer at the start, then argued for three days over the role of Melchizedek in the Book of Genesis. Unsurprisingly, after what Gray describes as *'a good deal of quibbling and tedious altercation'*[4] which never seemed to get anywhere, everyone was bored, tired and irritated, the gentry were unimpressed with their accommodation, the Reformed supporters thought that the townspeople of Maybole were sadly lacking in their hospitality, and one of them was heard to remark that *'if anybody brought bread and wine he would gladly accept it and care naught what it meant'*.[5] The debate ended with no conclusion when people voted with their feet. There are those who may feel that a template was set for theological debate in Scotland which has been adhered to ever since! The citizens of Maybole, who had never wanted the debate in the first place, gathered up all the books that had been brought by the Abbot for reference, and burned them publicly – another unfortunate precedent.

Quintin Kennedy died in 1564, and he was the last ecclesiastical Abbot of Crossraguel. Mary Queen of Scots had already granted the gift of the revenues of Crossraguel to George Buchanan, the leading Scottish historian and humanist who was to become the only lay Moderator of the General Assembly of the Church of Scotland in over four hundred years. Allan Stewart now became the commendatory Abbot of Crossraguel. This was a dubious though common practice whereby part or all of the revenue of a monastery was transferred to a patron, who received the income but fulfilled no duties of the Abbot's role, offered no spiritual oversight and was not even required to be resident or a member of the clergy; a kind of absentee landlordism. It was effectively used as a feudal form of reward or incentive to lay vassals.

Enter Gilbert Kennedy, the Fourth Earl of Cassilis, also known as 'the King of Carrick', such was his feudal power. By all accounts a most unpleasant character with previous form in land theft, and perhaps feeling a certain proprietorial inclination towards Crossraguel, Cassilis seized Allan Stewart, imprisoned him in Dunure Castle, and roasted him alive over an open fire until he agreed to sign over to him some of the land rights of the Abbey. Fortunately, Stewart was rescued by his brother-in-law, the Laird of Bargany, thus ensuring an ongoing feud between the two families. The Abbey of Crossraguel gradually declined, and is now under the care of Historic Environment Scotland. In an irony of history, in the late 19th century, a royal warrant gave the title of Abbot of Crossraguel to the Dean of the Chapel Royal in Scotland, currently the distinguished Presbyterian theologian David Fergusson.

***

If the 16th century in Scotland had seen religion bitterly and violently contested, the 17th century was even worse, as it was across all of Europe, where the Thirty Years War (actually a series of wars) between 1618 and 1648 was the deadliest religious conflict in European history. It killed around eight million people – a quarter of Europe's population – devastated the continent with famine and disease, bankrupted the protagonists and ushered in an era of horrendous witch-hunting. More than a century after the Protestant Reformation, emperors, kings, princes and rulers of numerous states were still wedded to the notion of religious uniformity, the belief that they had the right, and even the duty, to impose their own particular religious ideology and practices on their subjects, who had little choice in the matter. Though the focus was on religion, the impetus was also, and equally, political; it was about power, and the legitimacy and authorisation that religion gave to rulers. Nationalisms, ethnicities and identity were all used, abused and manipulated to gain support for one side or another, and large standing armies, often mostly consisting of mercenaries, made this a very dangerous strategy.

The conflict began when the Holy Roman Emperor tried to force his extensive domains into Roman Catholic uniformity, angering northern European Protestant states whose right to choose either Catholicism or Lutheranism as their official state confession had been granted in the 16th-century Peace of Augsburg. These northern states rebelled; Protestant Bohemians in Austria ousted the Hapsburg Emperor and elected their own new German monarch, Frederick V, Elector of the Palatinate of the Rhine. This in turn upset the southern, mostly Catholic states in the Empire, who retaliated by expelling the German Elector. Then Sweden weighed in on the Protestant side, closely followed by Catholic Spain seeking to crush Dutch Protestant rebels, and finally Catholic France, finding itself surrounded by imperial powers on its borders, joined the Protestant coalition. Here was the old French/Hapsburg rivalry for European pre-eminence stretched out across a whole continent.

Even for those well-read in military history, the details of the impact of the Thirty Years War are horrendous. Plague, pestilence, massacre, starvation, uprooted populations, bloodshed on a chilling scale and huge social trauma all bore consequences far into the future and far beyond Europe, as European powers extended their rivalries to their overseas colonies. In 16th-century Scotland, John Knox had taken great exception to what he called *'the monstrous regiment [rule] of women'*,[6] in particular that of Mary Tudor, the English Queen, and Mary of Guise, the Regent of Scotland. Who could read the history of the Thirty Years War without concluding that the regiment of men in the 17th century was far more monstrous?

Though not officially among the protagonists, Scotland was nevertheless involved in the Thirty Years War. The daughter of James VI and I, the Scottish king (and since 1603, the English king also), was Elizabeth of Bohemia, the 'Winter Queen', and she was married to the Elector Frederick V. Her fate was of great concern, and tens of thousands of Scottish soldiers fought in the armies of a dozen European states on both sides, particularly those of Sweden. But Scotland had its own wars to contend with, aspects of which mirrored those in mainland Europe.

Andrew Campbell, my six-times great grandfather, was born in 1680 at a time and place which was at the epicentre of a movement both religious and political, which embodied the conflicts which were tearing Scotland apart, and which put the country firmly in a pan-European context. The time was known as 'the Killing Time', the place was south-west Scotland, and the movement was known as Covenanting, whereby Scots sought to consolidate the Scottish Reformation of the mid-16th century, and to establish the Presbyterian system of government as the national church. But this was not a purely ecclesiastical matter. It was also a conflict between church and state, between church and crown, and between crown and state, and in the earlier part of the 17th century involved Scotland in what became known as the Wars of the Three Kingdoms, Scotland, England and Ireland.

In the 16th century, the Scottish Reformers had forced the Catholic Mary Queen of Scots to abdicate in favour of her son, James VI. Brought up as a Protestant, his leanings were towards the English Reformation system of episcopacy, which operated through bishops appointed by the monarch. He was unenthusiastic about a Presbyterian system which was less malleable to royal interference and fiercely independent in its governance. An earlier attempt to introduce bishops in Scotland had met significant resistance, and James was forced to concede church governance to the General Assembly of the Church of Scotland. However, following the Union of the Crowns, when James succeeded to the English throne and moved to London, he redoubled his efforts to introduce Anglicanism and episcopacy in Scotland, which remained deeply unpopular.

When his son Charles I became king, his unshakeable conviction that the divine right of kings gave him complete and unrestricted authority in every matter led to the attempt to impose religious uniformity and conformity on all the subjects of both Scotland and England, and he sought to introduce an Anglican liturgy, created by a group of Scottish bishops, to Scotland. This led to the drawing up of what became known as the National Covenant of the Church of Scotland. By this document, adopted and signed in Edinburgh, then copied and signed across Scotland, signatories were binding themselves in a religious oath to retain, uphold and defend the Presbyterian system, and to reject all innovations sought by the king, while still professing their loyalty to him. In 1640, the Covenant was adopted by the Scottish Parliament, and subscribing to it became mandatory on all citizens. This brought the Covenanters, as they were now known, into direct confrontation with the Established Church, and with Charles himself. In one of the many disastrous decisions which characterised his reign, Charles took military action against the Scots and was defeated by a Covenanter army in the so-called Bishops' Wars. When Charles, who was not keen on parliaments at all, nevertheless approached the English Parliament (many of whom were sympathetic to the Covenanters) for money to pay for his war against the Scots, they refused, refused to dissolve themselves and go away, and presented him with a long list of grievances and demands. This crisis led directly to the English Civil War.

The Covenanters were now effectively the government of Scotland. They sent an army to Ireland, to defend Scots settlers in Ulster from the Irish Catholics; following a request for support from the Puritan cause in England, they agreed to assist, on condition that the Scottish system of church government would be adopted in England (and Ireland). The Solemn League and Covenant between Scotland and England to that effect was drawn up, and Scotland sent an army into England to support the Parliamentarian side. But this brought about the outbreak of civil war in Scotland, as Scottish Catholics and Episcopalians took great exception both to fighting against the king, and to the imposition of the Covenant in Scotland.

You could grow very old trying to understand the history of religion in 17th-century Scotland. All the parties fell out with each other on several occasions. The Covenanters split, with each other, and with their English Parliamentary allies, and eventually Scotland was invaded by Oliver Cromwell's New Model Army, which defeated an army of Royalists and Covenanters who had buried their differences to repel an English invasion. Scotland was effectively annexed to England. The Church of Scotland lost all its civil power, and when Charles II came to the throne after the end of the Commonwealth, he renounced the Covenants, restored patronage (whereby the wealthy and landed were the ones who appointed the clergy, not the churches themselves) and brought back the bishops. The Abjuration Act of 1666 required anyone taking public office to swear an oath that they would not take up arms against the king, and rejecting the Covenants. Ministers who refused to recognise the authority of the bishops were to be removed from their churches.

This was a huge dilemma and crisis for the clergy, caught between pragmatism and principle. If they refused to swear, they would lose their livings, and any kind of influence in the Established Church. But if they did take the oath, they would be breaking an older and stronger promise, one which they saw as a covenant with God. Many refused; many left their churches of their own free will rather than wait to be ejected. The majority of these were in Ayrshire and the south-west of Scotland, a region with particularly strong Covenanting leanings. Now without church buildings to worship in, many ministers started to hold gatherings for worship and preaching in the open air, known as conventicles. The hills and moorlands of Ayrshire and the south-west are today dotted with stones and cairns, memorials marking where conventicles were held – and where those who attended them suffered severe fates. The death penalty was imposed on open-air preachers, many who attended were tortured, imprisoned, transported as bonded labour to the colonies, and some were just shot down without trial in the fields.

In an attempt to subdue this movement, which was seen by the monarch and Scottish government as open rebellion, the Duke of Lauderdale (the Lord President of the Privy Council, the effective rulers of Scotland at this point), all other efforts having failed, decided to send forces into the south-west to enforce the suppression of the conventicles. These included some Lowland militias, but mostly consisted of Highlanders (who became known as the 'Highland Host'), whose mythology went before them, and who were designed to strike fear into Covenanting hearts, being both mostly Gaelic-speaking Catholics and reputed to be wild barbarians. These forces were to be billeted in Covenanting communities, who were made responsible for feeding and housing them, and ordinary people in these counties were terrified that they would loot, plunder and commit atrocities. Lairds and landlords were held responsible for the actions and submission of their tenants and servants, but many of them were also resistant to the high-handedness of

Lauderdale and, by extension, the king, and as the conventicles grew larger and armed themselves, and resistance grew more widespread, they lacked confidence in their own ability to command obedience from their people. Their religious beliefs, but even more their politics, led to them becoming known as Whigs, the forerunner of the British political party that was to dominate in Scotland for the next two hundred years, and eventually became the Liberal Party.

A historian in the early 20th century wrote:

'The danger was increasingly imminent. It was plain that the West would yield only to coercion; both landowners and tenants in the shires were inclined to the covenanting party, and had, with few exceptions, refused to sign the Bond abjuring their nonconforming ways. Lauderdale, to whom nonconformity in religion meant disloyalty to the Crown and rebellion against all settled government, had determined that they must yield. To enforce his will, troops were necessary. The depleted state of the public treasury made it undesirable that these troops should come from without the borders of Scotland. In these circumstances, Lauderdale bethought him of the military forces of the clans, a source of warlike strength which many succeeding statesmen were to exploit.'[7]

The clansmen were led by their chiefs, among whom were many of the nobility of Scotland.

'On February 9th 1678, by letters sent from Ayr, he [the Earl of Cassilis] was ordered to publish on the next Sabbath day, at the market cross of Maybole and at all the parish church doors in his Baylery, a proclamation requiring all heritors, life renters, and others of the Baylery to appear before the Lords of the Committee at Ayr on the 22nd, to subscribe such bonds as should be appointed. In spite of the fact, however, that the Earl at once complied with this demand, and issued the proclamation as required, 1500 men were sent, on 10th February, into his district of Carrick

and took up free quarters there, most of them indeed, being billeted upon the estate of the Earl himself, the result being, as he complained, that "not onely free quarter, but dry quarter, plunder, and other exactions, with many insolencies and cruelties, too tedious and lamentable to report were committed".[8]

Over 250 signatories of the National Covenant had come from Maybole; all its ministers had refused to abjure. And in spite of his efforts to fend off the Highland Host, the Earl of Cassilis was not himself exempted. The Earl complained to the king, but it did him no good. The Committee of the West (those Lords appointed to oversee this military operation) *'maintained that at the time they had good reason to believe that the people of Carrick were in a state bordering on rebellion, that the Earl himself, the principal man in the district, had by his reluctant performance of his duties, been by no means an example to his people, and that it was most necessary to destroy all meeting-places of conventicles, since "there were far more armed men assembled in them almost weekly than could be represented by almost thrice the number of the standing forces".*[9]

The Committee then placed the same obligation on the heritors and leading citizens of the whole country of Ayr, naming twenty parishes, including Dalrymple. The Highlanders, extremely impoverished and undisciplined men, badly led, proceeded to loot everything they could carry away (Dalrymple was ordered to provide 40 horses) and generally insult their reluctant hosts. The parishes were ordered to surrender any weapons they might have. Eventually, having run out of plunder, and because their chiefs were worried that their Highland estates might be vulnerable to their own neighbours while the men were away, the Highlanders departed to make a gradual return north.

The horrors of the Killing Time did not end with their departure. There was in fact little bloodshed during this occupation; the local people adopted a tactic of passive resistance, not wishing to give Lauderdale or the king any excuse to mount a full-scale assault on the south-west. But armed risings by radical Covenanters in the south-west continued, the Highland Host returned and more executions followed. The Stuart line could not hold, and eventually, James II fled into exile. Through the Claim of Right Act of 1689, he was replaced by William and Mary as joint sovereigns. The Act of Settlement of 1690 finally established Scottish Presbyterianism, and the military engagements were ended.

Thousands of Scots died on one side or another in the Thirty Years War. Around 65,000 died in the Wars of the Three Kingdoms (and another 30,000 died of the plague during these years). Perhaps another 18,000 Covenanters died, in a country whose population was around 1.2 million. Scotland, for all its location on the extreme western edge of Europe, was fully participant in the continent's struggles and ideologies in the 17th century. The connection between the Holy Roman Emperor and Andrew Campbell of Piperston Farm, Dalrymple may seem tenuous and not immediately evident – but it's there.

It's there in the century of religious wars that brought death, disease, famine and terror to millions. It's in the long and bitter political battle between monarchies and aristocracies who used differing religious ideologies to claim the right to rule – and who may have sometimes actually believed in the theologies. It's in the theologies themselves, which elevated often minor and obscure aspects of religious texts into omnipotent and universal claims, and for which thousands died – and killed – not just for their own right to make these, but for the right to impose them on everyone else. It's in the struggle to affirm national identities when these were under severe threat, and in the power-games which deliberately set geographies and cultures against one another in the interests of the gamers. It's in the sincere conviction and desperation of poor and powerless people who glimpsed in their religion the possibility and promise of spiritual agency and equality when they had no agency or equality in any other part of their lives, and who were manipulated and betrayed by their monarchs, their landlords, their political leaders, their lawyers and many of their religious leaders. It's in the fact that at no time was this century democratic; neither women nor the vast majority of men had any say in its politics or its wars, though they were the ones who ultimately paid for them and suffered their consequences. This is the context Andrew Campbell was born into, and its fear, threat and loss could hardly have come any closer.

Andrew's father was an Ayrshire tenant farmer called John Campbell. There are several John Campbells who figure in Covenanting records; their stories include attendance at conventicles, pursuit as fugitives, arrest by another returned group of Highlanders led by John Graham of Claverhouse, known either as 'Bonnie Dundee' or as 'Bluidy Clavers' according to your perspective. Then imprisonment in the Covenanters' Prison in Edinburgh, escape, recapture, and for at least one of them, banishment to the American colonies. Shipped aboard the *Croune of London* were 257 prisoners in the most appalling conditions; but the ship foundered off Orkney in a storm, and 200 of them drowned, including John Campbell. Also drowned were many others from Ayrshire parishes, including George Hutchison of Straiton parish. Andrew's wife was Catherine Hutchison from Straiton. Were the couple both children of Covenanters? Well, these were both common enough Ayrshire names; there is no way now of knowing. But these must have been grim years anyway in Dalrymple, with many of the people being hunted as fugitives, harassed, occupied by soldiers, and numerous extrajudicial killings.

There is at least one other Covenanting link in our family. William Cunningham, my five times great-grandfather, was born in 1738 in Crawfordjohn, Lanarkshire, and was baptised into the Reformed Presbyterian Church in 1739. This very small Church emerged after the Act of Settlement as the continuation of the most radical of the Covenanting factions, the United Societies (often known as the Cameronians, after their founder, the field preacher Rev. Richard Cameron), who believed the Church of Scotland, and most Presbyterians, to have betrayed the Covenants. The United Societies frequently held their general meetings in the parish of Crawfordjohn, which had been a Covenanting stronghold; two women from there, Bessie Weir and Margaret Weir, had been arrested, imprisoned, and when they denied the authority of the king, transported to Barbados in 1687. The Societies' first ordained minister, Rev. John MacMillan, first preached and baptised in Crawfordjohn in 1706. The fact that William Cunningham was baptised into this church suggested a strong and continuing family adherence to this by now tiny Covenanting remnant. And there was a William Cunningham who was tried for treason in 1685 and banished to the Scots colony in East Jersey, New Jersey, transported on the *Henry and Francis*. Perhaps our William Cunningham was a descendant of his. Today, the Reformed Presbyterian Church in Scotland, fundamentalist in its Calvinism, survives with just five congregations.

After the religious conflicts came a series of bad harvests and devastating famines in the 1690s. For Andrew Campbell and Catherine Hutchison in Dalrymple, there must have been a great longing to reach a time of stability and security. But the new century, with the Union of the Parliaments of Scotland and England in 1707, brought about its own radical changes. In 1690, the re-Established Church of Scotland had been given the right of congregations to call their own ministers. But this right had been removed by the Patronage Act of 1712, passed by the British Parliament, which reintroduced the right of a 'patron', usually a hereditary member of the aristocracy or large landowner, to install the minister of his choice. The Act had been passed as a concession to induce the Scottish landed classes, who were often Episcopalian and sympathetic to the Jacobites (those who sought the return of the Stuart monarchy), to abandon their cause. The issue of patronage was to become a central one in the religious disputes of the 18th and 19th centuries.

In the rural areas, the Established Church continued to play a leading role not just in the religious beliefs of the people but in their civic life also. Each parish church was responsible for the provision of a church building, a minister and his stipend, and a manse including a piece of land known as a glebe. But it was also responsible for the provision of a school building and a schoolmaster's salary, and for ensuring that all the children in the parish had access to schooling regardless of means. It was responsible for relief of the poor, and the Kirk Session also acted not just as a church court but as a civil court. In particular, they were concerned with upholding social codes of sobriety, decency and respectability. This was essentially a conservative religious order, requiring conformity and uniformity and favouring hierarchical class structures; the local landlords were still the local power, and, as heritors in the parishes, they were responsible for the church finances. In practice, they were careful to minimise costs, or to pass them on to their tenants through produce and labour costs, the tenants in turn passing on the labour requirements to their farm servants and landless labourers. The lairds charged school fees, rental for church pews and fines for misbehaviour. In much of rural Lowland Scotland, the impact of all of this was to embed the church as the main agent of civil power. Religion was not a choice for people, adherence to it was the condition of their lives.

Andrew and Catherine, whatever their Covenanting history, were clearly in membership of the parish church in the first half of the 18th century. In 1743, one of their sons, also Andrew, was admitted to Communion:

'Dalrymple 3d Augt 1743

'This day [...] Andrew Campbell [...] came in to the Session and declared their sincere and hearty desire to Ratifie their Baptismal Engagements by partaking of the Sacrament of the Lord's Supper.

> *'Trial was taken of their knowledge and then they Received their tokens for the first time. This day was observed by this parish as the fast day in view of the Sacrament of the Lord's Supper.'*[10]

The younger Andrew was clearly a man of religious interests and theological literacy. In 1751, he subscribed to *'The Great Concern of Salvation: in three parts: viz. I. A Discovery of Man's natural State: Or, the guilty Sinner convicted. II. Man's Recovery by Faith in Christ: Or, The convinced Sinner's Case and Cure. III. The Christian's Duty, with respect to both Personal and Family Religion. By the late Reverend Mr. Thomas Halyburton, Professor of Divinity in the University of St. Andrews. The Second Edition. To which is prefixed, A short Account of the Author's Life. 2nd edn., 1751, HALYBURTON, Thomas. Glasgow, Kilmarnock.'* Halyburton was a Church of Scotland minister from a strong Covenanting family background, and his books are classics of Reformed theology still available today.

However, the experience of another son, Quintine, as recorded in the Kirk Session minutes of Dalrymple Parish Church in 1744, was possibly less of a cause for celebration:

> *'Dalrymple 26th Febry 1744*
>
> *'Margaret McMurtrie, Servant to Andrew Campbel in Piperstoune, came in to the session voluntarily and confessed she was with Child in fornication by Quintine Campbell, son to the said Andrew Campbell. She was Rebukt for her sin and Exhorted to Repentance, and cited apud acta to Compear before the Session next Sabbath. The officer is ordered to cite the sd Quintine to sd diet.'*
>
> *'Dalrymple 4th March 1744*
>
> *'Margaret McMurtrie and Quintine Campbell cited to this diet Compeared, and the woman's accusation being read in his hearing,*

he acknowledged the Charge. They were both rebuked for their Sin and exhorted to Repentance.

'NB That the sd Quintine Campbell and Margaret McMurtrie, some time after this appeared before the Congregation and pro-fessed their Repentance, were rebuked and absolved from the scandal.'[11]

Such public policing of sexual morality, which seems unthinkable to us today, was extremely common in Scotland for at least two hundred years. The Session minutes for Dalrymple are full of similar stories. A note in 1727 records what appears to have been the typical preoccupations of the elders:

'The Session appoint a meeting here upon Tewsday next for prayer and Refer the Consideration of any Scandals in the parish and Inspexion of the poor's Box, to that Diet; and in the mean-time order James Slowan and Marrion Campbell, who have formerly own,d their Guilt of fornication, to be cited to s[ai]d meeting.'[12]

Occasionally, the consideration of scandals in the parish (which have more than a hint of tabloid prurience about them) could be embarrassing to the elders themselves; in 1729, Duncan Campbell, the son of the church's Presbytery elder, was named as the father of her child, born out of wedlock, by one Janet Smith. There then follows a long account of the Session's efforts to hold Duncan (who had admitted that he was the father) accountable for his sin, to get him to do public penance and be rebuked. Duncan failed to turn up, then paid a fee to be able to sit in his own regular seat rather than in front of the whole congregation; finally, he and Janet both appeared, expressed their contrition, and were absolved. Crucially, Duncan was engaged by the Session to *'perform the duties of a Christian parent to the child'*.

'Fornication' was far and away the most common offence dealt with by Kirk Sessions; this was not a rare occurrence in small communities where people knew each other, as it never has been. It was almost always the woman who, for obvious reasons, was first apprehended. Her guilt could not be hidden. But though this whole process may have provided much voyeuristic glee for the 'unco guid', the self-righteous respectable, many of these, the elders and congregations, were themselves too personally involved for it to be entirely comfortable. Their own neighbours, sons, brothers, were participants, and one of the most frequent causes of pregnancy was a female servant being taken advantage of by her master or her master's sons. The fact that women were relentlessly harassed by Sessions to give up the name of the fathers without doubt owed much to narrowly patriarchal and punitive attitudes to women. But it also served as a way of holding men to account, of forcing them to admit their responsibility publicly, to acknowledge their children by providing some financial support for them, and by ensuring their baptism into the community of faith, regardless of their illegitimacy. In many regards, the parish church acted rather like an early version of the Child Support Agency.

Quintine Campbell and Margaret McMurtrie were my direct ancestors. Their son John was raised together with his half-brothers and sisters from his father's marriage four years later to Janet Rankine. John also farmed in Dalrymple, and was married for 66 years to Isabel Goudie, with whom he had ten children and 47 grandchildren. John and Isabel are both buried in Dalrymple Church graveyard, under a gravestone originally raised by John as a tribute of respect to his wife.

In 1834, the General Assembly of the Church of Scotland passed the Veto Act, removing the absolute right of landowners to appoint ministers to their parish. The Act gave male heads of families who were communicants with the parish the right to veto the appointment of a new minister if a majority of them objected. To this end,

ERECTED
BY
JOHN CAMPBELL,
LATE FARMER IN DANSTON AS A TRIBUTE
OF RESPECT TO THE MEMORY OF
ISABEL GOUDIE,
WHO WAS 66 YEARS HIS SPOUSE AND WHO
DIED FEB. 5TH 1831 AGED 87 YEARS.

ALSO OF
HIS SON JOHN WHO DIED MAY 20TH 1798 AGED 22.
HIS DAUGHTER CATHARINE WHO DIED JULY 9TH
OF THE SAME YEAR AGED 9.
AND HIS SON JOHN WHO DIED IN 1772,
AGED ONE YEAR.

JOHN CAMPBELL,
LATE FARMER IN DANSTON DIED SEPT. 27TH 1851,
AGED 88 YEARS.
INSCRIBED TO HIS MEMORY
BY HIS SURVIVING SONS.

the Assembly instructed Kirk Sessions to draw up rolls of the male heads of families in each parish. Hugh Campbell, one of the sons of John and Isabel, is on the roll for Dalrymple, so continuing the association with the Established Church.

Away to the north-east, and in a very different working context, John Johnston, the manager of the Duke of Hamilton's Redding Colliery in Polmont, was also identified as a head of family in the Church of Scotland parish. He was obviously sympathetic to the church's needs. Because the church itself was some distance away, too small, and according to the Statistical Account of 1845, written by the parish minister, *'damp, ill-arranged and most inadequate to the wants of the parish'*,[13] a preaching station had been established. This was served by a Church of Scotland probationer minister, and the services were held in the schoolroom of Redding Colliery. The schoolteacher for the colliery lived next door to John Johnston; presumably this was an arrangement they had agreed together.

And far to the west, on the island of Islay, where my forebears were weavers or worked on the land, the Established Church still held sway. Archibald Gilchrist, my great-great-great-grandfather, and the father of Marrion Gilchrist, was for forty-five years the parochial schoolmaster in Kilchoman, paid a stipend of £25 a year plus house and garden by the church. At the end of the 18th century, all the inhabitants belonged to the Church of Scotland. But it could hardly be said to be flourishing. A shortage of ministers who could speak Gaelic (still the mother tongue of the islanders) and too few church buildings for a widely-dispersed population in a place without good roads in the remoter areas did not make church attendance easy. The 18th century was a time of traumatic economic and social change for the Highlands and islands of Scotland. But the strength of Presbyterianism lay in the Lowlands, and neither the unshakeable theological certainties of the 16th-century reformers, nor the passionate conviction of the 17th-century Covenanters, spoke to the minds or hearts of Gaels, who had older loyalties. The Presbyterian system of government did not sit comfortably with a society being rent away from the clan system, and the religious and political wars and conflicts of the 17th and 18th centuries had often deliberately pitted Highlanders and Lowlanders against each other in mutual suspicion and cultural intolerance.

It's hard to look back on the religious history of Scotland from the 16th through the 18th centuries from an early 21st-century perspective without a considerable degree of horror at the immense amount of killing it involved, and from a Christian perspective, without an equal degree of shame. It is true of course that churches and Christians were all too easily co-opted by political and economic actors to legitimise and authorise their own interests (and what could be more persuasive than the claim to have God on your side). The efforts of the aristocratic and landed (and their battles with each other) to avail themselves of the land, wealth and civil authority of the Catholic Church were very successful in their appropriation of the revenue which John Knox intended to be used for the upkeep of the Kirk, the support of the poor and sick, the provision of work for the unemployed and for a publicly-provided school education for every child. The Reformers were perhaps naive in thinking that the support of the rich and powerful was motivated by religious piety; history should have informed them better.

Similarly, the struggle by the elites to contain and limit the absolute power of monarchs in the 17th century was not undertaken for the sake of the poor and powerless, whose own resistance and uprisings were given short shrift, regardless of religious affiliation. Universal suffrage was still the best part of three hundred years away, and the contested territory was the economic and political interests of the aristocracy and the landed gentry. The 'godly commonwealth' the Reformers had sought to establish contained within it much that was ungodly, and which seemed little influenced by the life and teachings of Jesus Christ on such central (one would think) values as forgiveness, reciprocity, compassion, kindness, humility, peacefulness and love. The zeal of the Reformers for the priesthood of all believers and the costly commitment of the Covenanters to freedom of conscience and spiritual equality was both limited ('all' never extended to all) and conditional (only the freedom to believe the same as us), and they sought to impose the same limits and conditionality as had been imposed on them.

In that regard, they seem to me to resemble the Russian revolutionaries whose belief that the end justifies the means eventually separated them entirely from any hope of achieving the end, and left only the mechanisms of control and power. And for women in particular, the mechanisms of control and power stretched from the intensely patriarchal, in which male authority was complete and women were entirely subject, to the profoundly misogynistic and punitive, and ultimately to the murderous holocaust of the witch trials. In these, religion bears more resemblance to present-day Islamic fundamentalism than anything else.

The structural constraints of any system – its laws, dogmas, justifications and pronouncements – do not ever tell us the whole story, of course. So much depends on where the story is being read from. And statements, speeches and legislation are sometimes a desperate and reactive attempt to control that which is uncontrollable and unpredictable – the actual behaviour and practice of human beings. For most men and practically all women, these centuries allowed them little agency and few choices, and where they did exercise these, punished them severely. Even where they didn't, they paid anyway – for other people's wars, wealth and power. But dissent was rising, and Scottish religion in the 19th century and beyond changed in ways that affected everyone, not least my own family.

Notes:

1. Desmond Tutu, original source unknown

2. Old Statistical Accounts for Scotland:
    https://stataccscot.edina.ac.uk/static/statacc/dist/home

3. ibid. 2

4. ibid. 2

5. ibid. 2

6. *The First Blast of the Trumpet Against the Monstrous Regiment of Women*, by John Knox, 1558

7. *The Highland Host of 1678*, by John Rawson Elder, J. Maclehose, 1914: https://electricscotland.com/history/host/index.htm

8. ibid. 7

9. ibid. 7

10. Dalrymple Kirk Session minutes: www.oldscottish.com

11. ibid. 10

12. ibid. 10

13. New Statistical Accounts of Scotland

Dissent, progressive pragmatism and social justice, 1872-2014

Within this lan' I'm verra sure
Full fifty sects are striving,
To keep the fools frae Satan's power
That hellward straight are driving;
But, as for me, I canna tell
Which ane o' them's the right ane,
That can the clouds o' sin dispel
That's sae apt to benight ane
                                   In open day.

(John Mitchell)[1]

My sister Lesley Orr, who shares the same family history, is a Scottish feminist historian and activist, whose doctoral studies were on women in Presbyterianism in Scotland, 1830-1930. She writes:

'In 1830, the Church of Scotland, established by the State, organ-ised on a parochial model, and with extensive involvement in the provision and administration of education and welfare, presented an apparently unitary face to the world. The Kirk, especially in the rural areas where most of the population still lived, was per-ceived as a cementing force in communities which tended to embody a static social hierarchy. Ministers were prominent and prestigious figures, both locally and nationally. Church affairs were considered to be of great importance. Religious belief and practice dominated the aspirations and fears of ordinary Scots. There was an identifiable Scottish Presbyterian ethos which seemed to give the nation its distinctive character.

'By 1930, after a century of division, the Church of Scotland was once more a unitary organisation, but with a much less central role – both practically and symbolically – in Scottish life. The intervening years had witnessed internal differences, Disruption, rivalry, and then the gradual piecing together of the shards of

Presbyterianism (though small fragments remained broken off).

'Even by 1830, however, the singular character of Scottish Presbyterianism was becoming pretty frayed. A tradition of dissent
dating back to 1733 had already established several hundred congregations which, at various times and for different reasons, had
seceded from the Established Church. These tended to be around
Fife and the west Central Belt, and were dominated by artisans
who found little opportunity for participation and power in a Kirk
dominated by the landed and professional classes. In 1847, various groups of seceders combined to form the United Presbyterian
Church; a denomination characterised by the Victorian values of
thrift, sobriety, pragmatism, and also a commitment to evangelical
and progressive causes. It nurtured a significant number of politicians, especially in the Liberal Party which dominated 19th-cen-
tury Scottish politics.'[2]

This description of Scottish church life during this period is exactly
the experience at the micro level of our own family. The Ayrshire
Campbells, settled and increasingly prosperous tenant farmers,
adhered to the Established Church for the best part of two hundred
years (and the part of the family that remained in Ayrshire may well
have done so for much longer). Their religion was part of the Moderate tendency in the Church of Scotland: conformist, tolerant,
willing to accommodate themselves to the landed and political elite
(who of course still owned the land they farmed) and the patronage
system.

It was only when Henry Campbell, son of John Campbell and
Marion Farquhar, married Margaret McLellan, daughter of Adam
McLellan and Catherine Lyall, in 1872, that this loyalty shifted. Margaret, the daughter and granddaughter of artisans and merchants,
was a member of the United Presbyterian Church, and they raised
their family in this quintessentially Victorian middle-class denomination. It's interesting that it was Margaret's denomination that the

family adhered to rather than Henry's; one might have expected it to be the other way around in such an intensely patriarchal place and time as late Victorian Lowland Scotland. But by now, a whole constellation of factors – economic, political and ideological – which had combined to create the public/private 'separate spheres', and the increasing fetishisation of motherhood and domesticity, saw the increasing privatisation and individualisation of religion. In this, women had been designated a key part. From being regarded as an unruly and troublesome problem of religion, disobedient threats to good order and male authority (most acutely demonstrated in the persecution and murder of thousands of women as witches from the 15th through the 18th centuries), women, particularly middle-class women, were now to assume the role of protectors of private virtue and guardians of Christian values.

'Having confined all those virtues inappropriate within the market or the boardroom to the hearts of their womenfolk, middle-class men were then left free to indulge in all those unfortunate vices necessary for successful bourgeois enterprise. The fate of women and Christian selflessness having been thus bound together, the dependency and social powerlessness of the first became the vir- tual guarantee of the social irrelevance of the second: once God had settled into the parlour, Mammon had free range in public life, and the exclusion of women from virtually all areas of public existence guaranteed that the tidy division was maintained. An ideal of femininity which combined holy love with social subordi- nation not only served to suppress women, it also tamed and con- tained the anti-capitalist implications of Christian love itself. Domestic Christianity, like domestic womanhood, was the most comfortable kind for bourgeois men to live with.'[3]

For Margaret, as for so many Victorian women, early widowhood at the age of 46 meant that this tidy division broke down somewhat. As the head of the family, and breadwinner for five children, three of whom were still at school, she was inevitably pulled into the public sphere. The characteristics of the United Presbyterian Church, and doubtless even more the personal support it offered, saw her continue her membership when she was living in Glasgow. It was probably through one of the many West End United Presbyterian churches (four within a half-mile radius) that the Campbells first came into contact with the Orr family.

James Fleming Gordon Orr, grandson of the Netherton grocers, having been privately educated in Helensburgh and Glasgow (a sign of how successfully this family had ascended into the middle class), studied theology in Glasgow, and became a minister in the United Presbyterian Church in the rural area of Ladykirk, Berwickshire, in 1897. He remained there for five years, then moved with his family to Otago in the South Island of New Zealand, a stronghold of Scottish-originated Presbyterianism, where he taught Greek and Hebrew until 1910, and was minister of Kaikorae Presbyterian Church in Dunedin. James then returned to Scotland and became the minister of St Margaret's Parish Church in Broughty Ferry. The UP Church had by now united with the Free Church (those churches which had left the Church of Scotland in 1843 during the Disruption), to form the United Free Church, but James was now returning to the Established Church. This necessitated his spending time as a probationer assistant minister in Edinburgh. He remained in St Margaret's until 1921, with the exception of some time spent in military service from 1917. Though he was by this time 45 years old, he was called up as a reservist; this was common towards the end of World War I, and he served as an army chaplain. In 1921, James moved again, this time to Africa, when he was appointed to be the minister of St Andrews Church of Scotland in Nairobi, Kenya, now part of the Presbyterian Church of East Africa. He was its first minister, and remained there until his death in 1935.

James's brother, Robert Alexander Orr, my grandfather, also became a Church of Scotland minister, and was ordained in 1910.

His ministry was considerably less far-flung than his brother's; after serving as an assistant minister in Dumfries, he became the minister of Dalreoch Parish Church in Dumbarton, a town on the River Clyde a few miles west of Glasgow, in 1911. Dumbarton is an old town, formerly the capital of the ancient kingdom of Strathclyde for several hundred years in the first millennium CE, built round the massive volcanic Dumbarton Rock, a fortified settlement attacked on numerous occasions. A former Royal Burgh, it's now the county town of West Dunbartonshire. Throughout the 20th century, Dumbarton was an industrial town, dominated by shipbuilding, and badly affected by the Depression of the 1930s. Its shipyards were heavily bombed by the German air force during World War II. Having seen his parishioners through two world wars, Robert retired in 1945, having spent his whole ministry in Dalreoch.

Robert married my grandmother Marion Campbell (always known as May) in 1911 in Craigrownie Parish Church in Kilcreggan. I have a vivid recollection of my grandmother describing how, after the wedding, she and her new husband were driven round the Gareloch to Dumbarton in a pony and trap, and that the driver had white ribbons fluttering from his whip. It's a thirty-mile drive through beautiful countryside, and they were married at midsummer. Today, their romantic drive would take them right past the extensive sprawl and barbed-wire of Faslane Naval Base, the location of the UK's nuclear weapons capacity; nuclear submarines armed with Trident missiles.

Robert and May raised four sons in Dumbarton, who all went to Dumbarton Academy, were enthusiastic sportsmen (becoming life-long supporters of Dumbarton Football Club, known as the Sons, from 'the sons of the Rock'), and went on family holidays every year to the Clyde island of Arran. All four of them served in the armed forces during the Second World War. David, the eldest, who had already followed in his father's footsteps and been ordained as a Church of Scotland minister, served as an army chaplain on the

Western Front from 1941-46, and took part in the liberation of Western Europe. The second son, Robert, was a Second Lieutenant in the Argyll and Sutherland Highlanders. The third son, Lyall, joined the Fleet Air Arm (the branch of the Royal Navy responsible for the operation of naval aircraft). The youngest son, my father Jack, trained as an aircrew navigator and bomb-aimer in the RAF.

How difficult and worrying it must have been for their parents to have all four sons away, especially after Robert (always known as Bertie) was declared missing in Malaya. The Second Battalion of the Argylls fought the Japanese in jungle warfare the full length of Malaya and held the causeway into Singapore. The whole battalion became prisoners of war of the Japanese in February 1942 after the final battles of Singapore. Bertie was captured on 21 December 1941, soon after the Japanese invasion, and imprisoned in Pudu jail in Kuala Lumpur, in conditions that were utterly grim. He died there of dysentery on 9 July 1942, and he is buried in Kuala Lumpur. He was 25 years old. His best friend at Dumbarton Academy, Rev. Duncan Finlayson, told me many years later with tears in his eyes, that Bertie was an outgoing, popular and charming young man, a lover of life. It seems appropriate that written on his grave are the words: *Beloved by all who knew him*. For the rest of her life, my grandmother kept a framed photograph of him, handsome in his full regimental uniform, by her bed.

Before the war, Bertie had worked as a stockbroker; after the war, Lyall and Jack (as my father was always known) both followed their father and brother into the ministry of the Church of Scotland. Following ministries in East Kilbride and Hamilton, Lyall moved with his family in the 1960s to work with the Presbyterian Church in Canada in St Andrews, New Brunswick, a small coastal town close to the border with Maine in the United States. Sadly, he died in a road accident in 1969; his family still live in Canada.

In the immediate post-war years, the brothers first came into contact with a movement which was to have a profound impact on at least two of them. The Iona Community had its genesis in Govan in Glasgow during the bleak years of the Depression of the 1930s. Govan had been the centre of Clydeside's shipbuilding industry, but had suffered considerably during the Depression. George MacLeod, the minister of Govan Old Church of Scotland, seeing the unemployment, insecurity and deep poverty in his working-class parish, realised that people there found the church to be far removed from their daily struggles. They felt that there was one set of rules for Sundays – going to church, saying your prayers, being 'respectable' – and another set for the rest of the week, in which poverty, oppression and injustice was simply ignored. They did not feel they belonged. The life of the church and the life of the world had drifted dangerously far apart, had become alien to each other. The common life of church and community had become fragmented and broken. MacLeod, a charismatic and visionary Highlander of enormous energy, sought ways that might help to bridge that gap.

MacLeod came to believe that part of the problem lay in the way that the clergy were trained. They were removed into theological colleges and seminaries, educated into a language and way of life that was far removed from that of the people they would return to minister to, and which was also far removed from the direct and vivid teaching of Jesus through parable, story and images drawn from the daily life and work of farmers, fishermen, housekeeping and husbandry. He saw a way in which two very different needs might be addressed – the needs of the unemployed joiners and welders of the shipyards for a job, and the need for clergy to find new ways of communicating and living the gospel.

In 1938, he recruited a group of young ministers who had just finished their theological training, and unemployed workers from the industrial Central Belt, to travel together to the remote Hebridean island of Iona, place of the Irish Christian mission of St Columba or Columkille, which had Christianised Scotland in the 6th century. There, they would work together on rebuilding the ruined monastic buildings around the ancient Cathedral. The ministers would work as the labourers for the craftsmen, the craftsmen would bring their perspective to theological and scriptural discussion, and all would live a common life of daily prayer, work and recreation. After the summer together, the craftsmen would either continue the rebuilding or return to the cities, while the ministers would go in teams to the poor urban parishes of central Scotland with this experience of community to assist them.

It was an imaginative and inspiring scheme, and indeed the Iona Community did rebuild the Abbey, and a common life. Many writers have dramatised these early events vividly – the physical rigours (they lived in huts and had no electricity), the awkward conversations, the growing bonds of friendship. Especially after the war ended, leaving a fragmented and broken country and continent, the original task of rebuilding the monastic ruins of Iona Abbey became a sign of hopeful rebuilding of community in Scotland and beyond.

Young people in particular were drawn to what was happening on Iona to volunteer on the rebuilding. A very generous donation given expressly for the purpose of developing the Iona Community's youth work, both on Iona and Mull and on the mainland, in conjunction with the Church of Scotland's Youth Committee, led to the establishment of youth camps on Iona, and the setting up of a youth house in Glasgow. This house, at 214 Clyde Street in Glasgow, became the Glasgow home of the Iona Community for thirty years. In a large building which included a restaurant, a chapel, a library and meeting spaces, a lively and full programme of religious exploration and radical politics was established, using street and community theatre, publications, educational and training classes to engage a wide range of people – young workers, students, trade unionists – and to set up and support many social and civic groups. Local activism was encouraged, and as a house of hospitality also, Community House was a refuge for people with addictions, homeless people and victims of violence.

David Orr, familiar from his own upbringing in Dumbarton with the industrial context and the urban poverty, was attracted by the vision of the Iona Community, and became its senior youth adviser, working and living with his wife Dora, a teacher, and their young family in Community House, running youth camps on Iona in the summer and programmes in Glasgow in the winter. This formative experience went with him in 1950 to his first parish, St Columba's Church in Burntisland, Fife, also then a shipbuilding town; the church was the first post-Reformation church in Scotland, built in 1592. But after the intense social engagement and outreach of David's work with the Iona Community, he felt a degree of frustration with the institutional church, which seemed to him to put too much effort into maintaining itself, while groups set up to deal with major life issues were ignored:

> 'If they pack up, nobody cares; this is incidental. Christian Aid Weeks, Refugee Years, nuclear disarmament campaigns, African issues – things which might conceivably bear some relation to our unity in Christ; well, it's only those of us who are particularly resilient and thick-skinned who can face the continual strain of raising such issues. The Church (by and large, except for a few) just isn't interested; or when they are accepted as part of the job of the Church they're far down on the agenda, and given the fag-end of our energy, and of our planning, and of our money.'[4]

In the midst of his frustration, David noted two things which inspired him: the growth of house churches, where the word and the faith was shared in people's homes, and the development of a corporate sacramental liturgy which enabled community to be seen around the holy table. From Fife, David returned to Glasgow in 1960, as minister of Govan Old parish, the church from where George MacLeod had founded the Iona Community, where he remained until his retirement in 1980. When he died in 1993 his obituary in the *Glasgow Herald* said this about him:

'He held no senior posts in the Church, but had great influence on the way in which it now sees itself serving the community. In Govan from 1960 until 1980, Mr Orr was involved with a number of local organisations, including the New Govan Society, which he established and which pioneered public participation in the planning process. Through it, a number of organisations of national importance were established, including the first commu-nity-based housing association in Scotland, Central Govan (now Govan Housing Association).'[5]

A primary aim of the New Govan Society was to encourage greater community involvement in the redevelopment of Govan, and Govan Housing Association became the model for the development and growth of Housing Associations in Scotland. The passion for com-munity-building and local participation and empowerment was a marker of his whole ministry, as it was for Jack.

Invalided out of the RAF, he had trained for the ministry in Glasgow, joined the Iona Community in 1949, and worked for two years as assistant minister with Iain Reid, another Community member, in the Old Kirk in West Pilton, a housing scheme in Edin-burgh. Following six years as parish minister in Kirkconnel, a former mining village (and Covenanting stronghold) in Dum-friesshire, he moved to be the first minister of St John's Oxgangs, another new housing scheme in the south of Edinburgh. He remained there for thirty years, retiring in 1987. He, like David, used the model of house churches and sacramental corporate liturgy to encourage and sustain the full participation of lay Christians in an outward-facing, community-oriented ministry.

My brother David Orr, who followed his uncle David's passion for housing justice in his own career, and who recently retired as the Chief Executive of the National Housing Federation (the umbrella body for housing associations in England), wrote:

'I grew up in a place called Oxgangs. It was a new council estate built on the south side of Edinburgh, halfway up the Pentland Hills. It was built in the late '50s and early '60s – one of a large number of new communities created around then.

'My father was the minister of a Church of Scotland church, St John's. We were there right at the start, even before the church was built, when services were held in a wooden hut on the site. My younger sister was the first baby baptised there.

'At that time, Oxgangs had a parade of shops, a school, a pub and a church. The community centre followed some years later, the library later still. My father, Jack, took the view that the church was not just for the people who came to services but had a key role to play in the life of the whole community. He set about, with lots of help from my mother Janet and various other people in the church, to make that a reality.

'I guess Oxgangs was in many respects a fairly unremarkable place. The homes were good quality and spacious, even if lacking in architectural merit. Most were council homes to rent with some for people to buy. There was also an area we all called, with startling literacy, the 'self-builds'. It was only in my mid 40s that I discovered this was the biggest single self-build estate in the country. The school and particularly the church became the centre of a vast array of community activities and my dad was known by everyone. I still assert he was the best community worker I have ever met with a fantastic ability to get people to do things they themselves didn't think they could do.'

The influence of growing up in this church and this community was profound, and has shaped my whole life; not just professionally, but politically, culturally and spiritually. St John's was opened in 1957, built as part of the Church of Scotland's Church Extension programme to serve the new communities springing up around Edinburgh, and it was a youthful place; in the days before much else was there, the church was very important for many young families who had moved there from other parts of the city. Local resident Peter Hoffman, in his book about growing up in Oxgangs, has happy memories:

'I recall with great fondness the St John's Church Fete held annually each June – it really was a highly enjoyable day out. Looking at the area of the church it couldn't have been that large, but in my mind's eye it remains so. I vividly recall the bendy "electric wire" (battery-operated) that one tried to take a handle with a ring on the end from the start to the finish without the buzzer sounding – not often achieved as it took a steady hand – certainly beyond me today as it was at the time.

'The ice cream sold was always very pleasant and … they held a sprint race for boys and girls on the grass area adjacent to the church building – I still recall receiving a colouring book and paints as a prize. There were excellent stalls selling all sorts of serendipities – it was from here and long before eBay we garnered our knowledge of ancient Dandy and Beano annuals.

'They always seemed to be very lucky with the weather; they really were sunny occasions and the volunteers – presumably church goers – were equally sunny in their disposition, smiling and friendly – a really great and lovely day out for all the family.

'Similarly, I also recall performing in local youth club drama productions at the church hall – it was also probably one of several venues for The Pentland Festival …

'One of the loveliest memories of living at Oxgangs between 1958 and 1972 was the sweet sound of the St John's Church bells which

rang out every Sunday morning calling the parishioners to wor-
ship. They had a lovely tone to them, somehow fresh and inviting,
but also serving as a reminder of church bells down the centuries
too ... Writing this has just given me the idea to record the sound
of the St John's Church bells before they are perhaps silenced for
ever.[6]

Scotland has been marked by a sad sectarian history, but in these heady days around the Second Vatican Council, the leadership of all the local churches were ecumenically committed – to a new area, a new openness, a new start. Regular shared worship, the conviviality of celebrations, shared meals and hospitality, study groups and house churches, ecumenical pilgrimages and holidays, and, most importantly for me as a teenager, the ecumenical youth group, with a focus on justice and peace activism and witness, were, profoundly, an ecumenical formation, of active engagement with the local community and with the wider world.

That early formation, I have come to realise, was far from the norm. As a teenager, the youth group gave our youthful idealism and desire to change the world a place to be practically engaged, to learn the beginnings of a solidarity that went beyond our own self-interest, to be with adults who practised what they preached, and who took us teenagers seriously, treated us with respect, and helped us to believe that we could make a difference. Adolescence can be an awful time, a knife-edge, and today, in a context in which society is fearful of its youth, and loads them with huge financial burdens, and in which the church has often retreated from youth work, I look back with gratitude to the adults who engaged with us on our knife-edge.

There are several things in particular that were characteristic of church life. The first of these was its creativity. This predominantly working-class church was a hub of people making things. Making delicious food for many kinds of celebrations, or baking for many kinds of fundraisers; making music of many kinds, famously in the guild concerts, but also children's concerts, singing in hospitals and care homes, singing new hymns in church, and my own favourite memories include carol singing by the light of flaming torches through the streets of Oxgangs in the snow, and an unforgettable, and somewhat uncharacteristic, performance by my father, wearing a dress and a curly wig, as 'the lady that's known as Lou'. Bringing skills of carpentry, decorating, needlework, knitting, the list goes on and on, and I think, encouraged many, many people, not least children and young people, to believe in their own gifts, have them affirmed, and go on to develop and share them in other contexts. And for me, a learning of how much more enjoyable these things are when we do them together, and for the common good.

Creativity too in worship and prayer, using drama, art, dance, poetry and above all testimony in the sharing of the story of faith and proclaiming the gospel. I am only one among many who gained their first experience of speaking in public, at a young age, in helping to lead services in St John's. Reflection and prayer too, in house groups and reading the Bible in community, in celebrating the high and holy days of the Christian Year with other Christians from the neighbouring Catholic and Episcopal churches; all ways of deepening our discipleship and strengthening us for the challenges of daily living.

Nor was it ever an inward-looking church, focussed only on its own life. It looked out to the world which Jesus called his followers to serve. Sometimes this was local: in supporting a whole range of community groups – preschool playgroups, senior citizens, uniformed youth organisations; in arranging meetings with local politicians and planners, and not least, in encouraging individual members in their own involvement. Sometimes the community-building was global; in house-to-house and other fundraising and awareness-raising for Christian Aid, and in welcoming visitors from other parts of the world.

For nearly sixty years, this was a community caring for one

another through illness and bereavement, in family struggles and work problems, but also in celebrating and sharing the joys as well as the sorrows, the triumphs as well as the tragedies, the arguments as well as the agreements.

Oxgangs is a different place today from the new, young area just being established with high hopes in 1957, and the church, begun in a hut, has been a faithful witness ever since. Today Oxgangs is a settled and ageing community, and the local churches to some degree reflect that. But I think that these fruits, of creativity, community and care, are not just all in the past. They live on, and bear new fruits, in the lives of many still in Oxgangs, but of far more people scattered to all corners of our country and of the world. To bear witness to a generation, which is effectively what St John's did, was no small thing, and its harvest is beyond our knowing.

In 2014, St John's Church closed. Peter Hoffmann wrote about the closure in the *Scotsman* newspaper in January 2017:

'Hogmanay 2014 was the first occasion in 56 years that the church bell did not ring out over the festive period. The church closed and the congregation amalgamated with Colinton Mains Church to form St John's Colinton Mains Church. Even more devastating for many, however, is that the former St John's Church, Oxgangs has now been demolished. Whilst the community was aware it was imminent, seeing the photographs of it happening took your breath away. Within the grey urbanity of Oxgangs three fine buildings had stood out: The Riach-designed St John's Church from 1957; the strikingly Modernist St Hilda's Church, from 1965 – also razed to the ground – and the remaining St John's Colinton Mains Church. These buildings anchored and rooted the community. They helped to provide a sense of community and were an important link with the past. And if no longer the beating heart of Oxgangs, they were still AT the heart of Oxgangs.

'Because whenever you passed by, the buildings triggered memories. Not just memories of church going and the key stages of life – the christenings, the weddings and the funerals – but all the community events that were held there over the past half century. "I loved the clean and elegant lines, the combination of warmth and light, the fantastic chancel space. It spoke so eloquently of the spirit of optimism, hope for the future, participation of all, and community building which characterised the best of Oxgangs in the 1960s and '70s."

'The church bell itself came from the Trinity College Church in Jeffrey Street and previously was one of Edinburgh's town bells, rung out each morn and at evening-tide. It was cast in the Netherlands in 1632. The sound of a church bell ringing out signifies something important. For when poet John Donne spoke of 'For Whom the Bell Tolls, It Tolls for Thee', it does indeed, *because when something dies we all die a little. I guess what he was really saying was that whatever affects one, affects us all.'*[7]

And for my brother David, the demolition moved him to reflect on the nature of community today:

'Things like this lead to reflection. I don't think I am just feeling nostalgia for my childhood, although that is probably part of it. My anxiety is about what happens when institutions that are part of the fabric of communities disappear. We all need such institutions, populated by people who turn places from a large number of disparate households into a collective identity where we feel connected and rooted. Many churches of different faiths and denominations still play this role.

'And one of the reasons I love my connection to housing associations is that I see many of them playing this critical role. In a time where the nation feels pretty divided, this kind of community

connectivity genuinely is critical. We have to ensure that housing associations and others retain the potential to do this job.

'*My other reflection is that Oxgangs worked. There were problems and challenges and many people who were poor and who struggled. But in the main it was a safe and secure place to live, with good-quality and genuinely affordable homes. It was an optimistic place and time. In the 1940s Oxgangs was green fields. By 1960 it was home to 7,000 people. It was built at a time when there were visionary people who understood that slums had to be cleared, the wounds of the war had to be repaired and we had to plan for a growing population.*

'*We don't, thankfully, have the same kind of slums now and we don't have a landscape scarred by bombs any longer. We do, though, have a growing population and a genuine crisis in our ability to meet that need.*

'*We need visionary people again who are not scared of building at scale and who want to create the kind of community that Oxgangs became. We need new places that can provide my children and grandchildren with the stability and security that a good home in a supportive community can provide. We need institutions like St John's that are a centre, a beating heart, and we need people like Jack and Janet (and there are thousands of such people all over the country) who care enough to make these places work. Our collective ability to build great new places to live cannot only be part of our past. It has to be our future too.*'

I followed my father and grandfather in studying divinity at Glasgow University (I remember the slight shock I felt on finding my sober and law-abiding father's name carved in his small and unmistakable handwriting into a lecture-room desk), served as assistant minister in the Church of Scotland parish church in Muirhouse, an Edinburgh housing scheme, and was ordained in 1977, one of the first dozen or so women ministers. My working life has actually mostly been spent working for ecumenical organisations, including the Iona Community and Christian Aid, as well as periods spent working outside the church altogether.

My early experience located me in a wider vision of human family and I can no more not belong to it than I could not belong to my birth family. Over many years, the values I learned then – of inclusion, equality, respect, hospitality and justice – have continued to be stretched and enlarged. This has never been a simple or painless process. It has encompassed activism in many social movements, and a commitment to campaigning and political engagement first shaped in Oxgangs.

The community demonstrated in St John's, Oxgangs, is not unique. Over my professional life, I have done a great deal of travelling, visiting and working with an extraordinary variety of groups within, outside and on the margins of the Christian church. Much of that has been within Britain and Ireland, and from many Christian traditions and none. They have been people gathered in intentional communities and house churches, in women's networks and interfaith groups, around local and national issues and campaigns, in community organisations and prayer groups, around festivals and magazines and arts events, in student and chaplaincy groups, in Churches Together and in dozens of local churches. It has felt like an extraordinary privilege to share so broadly, if briefly, in the life and faith of so many people.

None of these churches, groups or organisations is perfect, and many of them struggle to maintain a disciplined life of faith with few resources, little recognition and in the face of some institutional disapproval. Many of them are found in the poorest communities. Their ideas have often been received with indifference, the training and skills they have has not been used, their good faith questions have never been answered, their abilities have been overlooked. But they have hung in there as part of the church, and I honour them.

They are ecumenical, in the broad sense. Because their focus and concern are primarily life and work rather than faith and order (to use the theological terms) their inclusiveness is that of those who share praxis, and they are tolerant of doctrinal differences, in which anyway they have less investment than those holding denominational power, or those whose religion is primarily ideological and propositional. They place more emphasis on belonging and behaving: 'by their fruits you shall know them'.

They are deeply engaged in civic society, which they see as the appropriate place for the expression of neighbourly love. And because they have a vision of the common good as extending beyond the borders of their own national state, they have an ability to offer a genuine and practical welcome to refugees and asylum-seekers which goes well beyond the suspicious and grudging governmental ones, and the hysterical hostility of tabloid newspapers. A different story about who is my brother, my sister, underlines a quiet but passionate commitment to justice in trade, in international debt and in human rights. Nor is this care confined to far away. These are people who run lunch clubs, parent and toddler groups, Senior Citizens organisations and neighbourhood schemes, organise and volunteer with support projects for homeless people, people with physical and mental health problems, survivors of domestic violence and sexual abuse. They raise money for a wide range of church and community initiatives. They foster and adopt children, and offer support, counsel and encouragement to family and friends.

They are people in whom a quiet spirituality and faith commitment is found. They don't spend any time trying to prove creationism or the corrupting effects of homosexuality on the nuclear family. They are people who, with little fuss and with great kindness, thoughtfulness, humour and patience, refuse to countenance the dehumanisation of their fellow human beings on account of their race, religion, sexuality, class or gender. Their common life is characterised not by any desire for popular relevance, but by a humble and faithful desire to love God, whom we cannot see, by loving our neighbour whom we can see. In a cynical and sectarian world, they represent Jesus to and for me.

I honour them, and at the same time, I see that this way of being the church is passing away. According to the Church Statistics survey in 2015, UK Church membership has declined from 10.6 million in 1930 to 5.5 million in 2010: or, as a percentage of the population, from about 30% to 11.2%. By 2013, this had declined further to 5.4 million (10.3%). If current trends continue, membership will fall to 8.4% of the population by 2025. All the mainstream Christian denominations have seen significant falls in membership, with the fall being greatest in Scotland (although, somewhat confusingly, church attendance still remains higher in Scotland).

And as I look back over more than three hundred years of church membership in my own family – from the radical Covenanter William Cunningham in Lanarkshire to the Establishment Campbells in Ayrshire, from the quintessential Victorian progressive pragmatism of the MacLellans in the United Presbyterian Church to the community and social justice orientation of the Iona Community-influenced Orrs – I recognise that this important strand of our family story is coming to an end, and that after me, there will probably be no more ministers, and little or no connection with the institutional church. Why I think this, is another part of the story.

Notes:

1.   John Mitchell, from 'A Braid Glow'r at the Clergy' in *Radical Renfrew: Poetry in the West of Scotland from the French Revolution to the First World War*, ed. Tom Leonard, Polygon, 1990

2.   Lesley Orr Macdonald, from *A Unique and Glorious Mission: Women and Presbyterianism in Scotland 1830-1930*, Lesley Orr Macdonald, John Donald Publishers, 2000. Used by permission of Lesley Orr

3.   ibid. 2

4.   From *Chasing the Wild Goose: The Story of the Iona Community*, by Ron Ferguson, Wild Goose Publications, 1998

5.   *Glasgow Herald*, 1993

6.   Peter Hoffmann, *Oxgangs: A Capital Tale*, Peter Hoffmann, 2022. Used by permission of Peter Hoffmann

7.   Peter Hoffmann, *Scotsman*, January 2017. Used by permission of Peter Hoffmann

Life and learning, 1815-2020

A tale of two grandmothers

When I count my blessings, as I do quite frequently, very high on the list is the fact that I can read. Literacy has given me access to education, information and enjoyment; it has enabled me to study, to earn a living, to use my imagination and creativity. I can read the instructions on medication, directions for travel, recipes, planting information on seed packets, the daily news, stories to my grand-daughter. It is a blessing I try never to take for granted.

I became an enthusiastic reader at the age of five, and thereafter spent much of my childhood with my nose in a book. This caused a degree of family conflict, since it tended to interfere with my share of the household chores, my ability to get to school on time in the morning (having been awake half the night reading under the covers) or even to get home without injury, given my tendency to walk into lampposts or bump into other pedestrians; reading while walking is not a new phenomenon, though I did it with a book not a phone. My favourite place was the public library, which I visited several times a week, and I remember a cousin asking me incredu-lously if I really ate books – she had heard her mother describe me as a bookworm. My second favourite place was the public library in Helensburgh.

> *I remember, I remember*
> *the first time I visited Helensburgh Public Library*
> *(staying with my gran);*
> *the wood panelling,*
> *the musty smell,*
> *the sun falling along the floor*
> *in long shafts of shimmering dust,*
> *and all those books!*
>
> *I thought I had arrived in heaven.*[1]

I think what I loved most of all about books was that they allowed me to venture into many new and different worlds, far removed from a quiet Edinburgh childhood, to share experiences I was never going to have, to visit places I never expected to see in times either long gone or far in the future, to encounter ideas that were unfamiliar and challenging. That's still what I read for, these other worlds.

I haunt first- and second-hand bookshops, charity shops and book sales. Where else could you find such riches for such modest outlay. This is a blessing I'm very happy to count. Learning and literacy have long been considered core Scottish values, even part of our national identity. We take pride in an early national educational framework and in the icon of 'the lad o' pairts'; in the traditional belief in educational egalitarianism, regardless of class. Well, yes and no. This is a story that needs a bit more examination.

Take my grandmothers. My grandmothers were very different. My father's mother, Marion Elizabeth Campbell (May), born in Albert Park, Kilcreggan in 1888, was a farmer's daughter and a minister's wife, and mother, and she lived a life very characteristic of women of her time and class. She never worked outside the home, but ran the manse in Dumbarton where my grandfather was the minister for 37 years, raised her family, baked for and often opened fundraising events, was a keen Guildswoman, visited parishioners and opened her home to innumerable visitors of every description. She saw her four sons go off to World War II, but only three come back, one of them lost in the jungles of Malaya. In her 20-year widowhood, she moved to a small house in Helensburgh, where she hosted family and friends, including her many grandchildren, travelled around the country, always on public transport, to visit in her turn, and died peacefully in bed at the age of 83.

She was a major influence on my childhood and on that of many others far beyond her family, to whom she was also known as Granny Orr. What I remember about her is that she was the most classless person I ever met. She treated everyone exactly the same, either as friends or as potential friends. She approached them with the same warmth and in the same manner and with the same expectation that they had only been waiting for this opportunity to tell her the story of their lives – which, to their surprise, most of them did. She cared not at all for her surroundings, but accepted each as yet another chance to talk to all the interesting people around her. Bus station, surgery, hospital, church, shop, street – she would talk to anyone anywhere. She fed them pan drops and cups of coffee out of her little flask and wrapped them around in the warmth of her complete attention to them. The most unexpected people poured out their troubles to her, and she listened and gave sensible, motherly advice. She never forgot a name, even of people she had met decades before, and the small details of family connections were the stuff of life for her, because they were just that, connections, the links that held people together, the threads that wove them into belonging in the web of life. She was a humble and gentle woman with an enormous talent for friendship, and she was a wonderful grandmother. She inspired me and encouraged me in everything I did, though my life and aspirations were very different from hers.

I say she was classless, and she was in her attitudes. But of course, beyond the interpersonal, her life was solidly rooted in the professional middle class. She lived in a large house on a hill (though, as it was a manse, it did not belong to them), next door to a doctor and his family. Every summer they rented a holiday house in Arran; she was a keen bridge player all her life. When I was a child living in Oxgangs, she regularly visited an old lady living in one of the council houses for senior citizens down the street from us who had been a maid in her home in the 1920s. And much to our rather horrified amusement as children, we learned that our father and his brothers had been wont to address their parents as Mater and Pater in their youth.

The embedded class structure in Lowland Scotland was most clearly visible in comparison with our mother's family. My mother's mother, Sarah Wallace Smith Morran Thomson, was a miner's wife born in Woodmuir, West Lothian in 1893. Her husband, Clement Johnston, died when my grandmother was still in her thirties, leaving her with seven children, five of them under the age of six, to bring up on her own in the days before the welfare state. Her life was one of fairly unremitting struggle; of going out to work as a cleaner, of poverty, worry, hardship and exhaustion. She died aged 56, when her youngest child was eighteen, her task accomplished. A hard life, yet I know that though she didn't laugh very often, when she did, her laugh was rich and infectious; that she played the piano at the cinema for the silent movies. She died just before I was born, but my life has been shaped in subtle ways by her history and the injustices implicit in it.

Sarah herself was the youngest of nine children. Her father and her six brothers were all coal miners; her mother died when she was eight years old at the age of 47 and one of her two sisters died of TB at the age of 20. She married my grandfather Clement Johnston in 1913 at the age of 19, just five weeks before their son John was born. Perhaps her memory of this was what made her fiercely protective of her daughters when they were in their teenage years; my mother described how, coming back very slightly late from a date with my father, they met Sarah out in the street looking for them, carrying the bread knife.

Sarah lost her eldest child when he was six years old. Her second child, another Sarah, died of tuberculosis at 28, another illness that disproportionately hit the poorest, leaving a young daughter, Sylvia, who was then brought up by her grandmother. My mother and her family did not have an inside toilet until 1947; for them, indoor sanitation was a luxury unavailable in the kind of rented accommodation they could afford. It was the post-war foundation of the welfare state and the National Health Service which gave millions of families like mine free maternal- and health-care and decent housing.

Sarah and Clement had six more children, five daughters and one son, born in 1933 just after the death of his father at the age of 47, and named after him. Sarah moved with her children into Edinburgh, first into a single-storey terraced house, originally built for flour mill workers in Haymarket, and then eventually in the 1940s to a flat in the new housing scheme of West Pilton. During the war, most of her children had been evacuated to the coast, to East Lothian. Serious German bombing raids led to thousands of Edinburgh families sending their children away from the city; my mother was sent with one of her sisters to two different hosts in the old mining town of Tranent. Their first host was an old woman who had had no children of her own, was quite unused to coping with them, and who my mother remembered as being always cross and nasty to them. Their second placement was more successful; they lived with the Town Clerk and his wife, who treated them very well. But it all must have been somewhat of a lottery, sending one's children to live with complete strangers in an unfamiliar place. Within a year, Sarah brought the girls home to Edinburgh; Clem, the adored baby and only son of the family, had never been evacuated.

In spite of the huge responsibilities my grandmother carried, she had no say in the political and economic decisions that shaped her life, and didn't get to vote until she was 33. She supported her family by working as a cleaner – a low status, low pay, insecure job at a time when there was considerable stigma attached to working women (though women had always worked), and a lack of jobs available to those who had no family connections, marketable skills or tertiary education.

The services that enabled my grandmother's family to escape poverty didn't just depend on their ability to work hard – God knows, they did that! They were possible because of a redistributive tax system which made essential services accessible to everyone in a fair way. In 1945, with the introduction of the Family Allowances Act, my mother's family began their long journey out of poverty.

My mother Janet was the youngest of the daughters and the first in her family to go on to higher education. Although they were all clever girls, all of her older sisters had to leave school and find work – this very poor working-class family could not afford for more than one of them to go to college. Visiting my mother's older sister in 2017, she spoke of having attained university entrance standard in her high school examinations, and her disappointment at being unable to take up a place. She was the last of her generation, and died shortly afterwards at the age of 89. My mother became a student at Moray House College of Education to train as a primary teacher; but romance intervened, and she married my father at the age of 19 in 1950. This necessitated her leaving college, but the guilt she felt at giving up the opportunity that had been denied to her sisters always bothered her. When her children were all at school, she returned as a mature student to Moray House, completed her training and taught in Edinburgh primary schools for twenty years. All four of her own children, boys and girls, went to university, assisted by the free and equal access to education available in the 1970s and 1980s.

In fact, my mother was the first woman to go into higher education on either side of my family. Though May Campbell married her minister and her three surviving sons all went to university, none of her own birth family, the Kilcreggan Campbells, was educated beyond secondary level. May left school at fourteen, and, following the prevalent pattern of middle-class girls of the early Edwardian era, would have expected to stay at home and help her mother run the household until her marriage. In the event, it was her sister she helped. Her oldest sister Catherine (Kit) had married a vet and gone to live in Worthing, where she gave birth to three girls in four years; May went to visit her for a fortnight and stayed for five years. I am sure that Kit must have appreciated the assistance – I know that my grandmother retained a particular affection for these three nieces, Peggy, Lexie and Mamie, whose early life she had shared.

Though both my grandmothers were literate, neither the middle-class one nor the working-class one had, nor expected to have, education beyond the age of fourteen. In the year 2000, a male historian, writing about higher education in Scotland before the 20th century, said: *'Entry to university was open to anyone (but not women and girls).'* Nothing like a masculine frame of reference for consigning half the population to invisibility and non-being!

As in many other arenas, what seems at first sight to be the democratic and inclusive history of Scottish education has hidden a far less egalitarian story, by dint of the deceptive (and drearily familiar) use of words like 'all', 'anyone' and 'everyone'. In reality, these words were heavily gendered. All meant 'all men'. The masculine was normative, and in education too, women and girls were problematised, supplicants seeking entry to a male world and inclusion in the definition of full humanity.

Lindy Moore, a scholar and researcher on gender history in Scottish education, writes on the impact of the Scottish Reformation on education: *'The Presbyterian church of the Reformers wanted a godly commonwealth, whose members knew their religious duties from close knowledge of the Bible, a theology that required a literate public of both sexes. By the 17th century, the core curriculum, which was expected to take about two years of study, consisted of learning to read and spell from the Bible, and the memorising of psalms, prayers, graces and the catechism. Schooling was "serious, earnest, harsh, utilitarian, ordered, dominated by a desire first to bring all to personal eternal salvation through instruction in reading".*[2] This curriculum sounds remarkably similar to that of the more extreme Wahhabi-influenced madrasas in some Muslim countries. But whether learnt at home or at school, this curriculum was similar for all social classes, and for both girls and boys.

In the 18th century, while most girls were taught to read, for many this was at a purely functional level. They had little access to books, few opportunities to use reading skills, and had to contend with moralising about what was unsuitable for them to read (more or less everything non-religious). Their ability to write was even more constrained, with estimates suggesting that 85% of women, compared with 35% of men, were unable to sign their own name. There was little of economic value to be gained from female writing skills; no women had jobs which required them. And while boys of all classes had the chance of going on to study more academic subjects in parochial or burgh schools, girls were directed to schools run by women teaching sewing and knitting, considered to be far more essential to their futures. These practical schools were almost the only place where women could work as schoolteachers. And of course, girls were barred from entry to the universities.

If economics was a primary reason given against educating girls in the 18th century, class became an increasing factor in the 19th century. The ideas of the Scottish Enlightenment saw a great improvement in the education of middle-class girls, with a broad curriculum and even, in some girls' schools, a particular emphasis on science; all of this was based on the notion of a new role for educated women as reformers and influencers of the family as wives and mothers, and was strictly limited to the private, domestic sphere.

However, many of these middle-class women, frustrated by the extreme and increasing demarcation of their lives into 'separate spheres' of public and private, took the opportunity to establish teaching or management careers for themselves by founding separate schools with a separate curriculum for working-class girls. These focussed on the same practical, domestic skills and the teaching of religion and morality; all of which might be expected to increase the supply of well-trained domestic servants with a satisfactory work ethic.

School attendance for both girls and boys was made compulsory from 1872. Standards for reading and writing were also equalised for both, but lower expectations for girls in arithmetic and compulsory needlework and cookery for girls (boys were forbidden to do this and directed instead to various kinds of wood- and metalworking) formalised and institutionalised a gender differentiation which was still in operation in my secondary school in the 1960s. Perhaps in an attempt to make cooking and sewing sound more aspirational for the girls who mostly disliked these subjects, they were referred to by the collective title of Domestic Science. In the 1970s, this title mutated into Home Economics; by the 1990s, my son was able to study Kitchen Technology. The titles seem to reflect the prevailing orthodoxies of the decades. Today, in my old school, Home Economics is still offered, in the Technologies department. I assume that boys may also now study this, and girls can study the current equivalents of technical drawing and woodworking.

The struggles of women to be accepted on an equal basis into higher education, and into the teaching profession, are perhaps not as well-known as women's fight to be able to train in medicine; but they share the same experience of having to confront profound misogyny, naked self-interest, pious platitudes and the spouting of the most extraordinary and impertinent rubbish. But change happens, even when it must do so against a background which was largely indifferent to the obstacles that had been faced by girls and women for centuries, and which did not count gender equality as a core value in its curriculums. By the mid-1980s, girls were achieving higher qualifications than boys in both Standard-grade and Higher exams, and by the end of the 20th century, girls of all social classes were outperforming boys of the same social class, all educational institutions were open to them, and women formed the majority of higher education students.

The University of Glasgow, which my grandfather and great-uncle attended at the turn of the 20th century, my father and uncles attended in the 1930s and 1940s, which I attended in the 1970s, and which my son, daughter, niece and nephew attended in the 1990s and 2000s, was founded in 1451. The first women were admitted as students to Scottish universities in 1892, 441 years later, and the first woman graduate was Marion Gilchrist, who was the first woman in Scotland to graduate with a medical degree. Today, almost 60% of the university's students are women, and its women graduates have been pathbreakers and innovators in many academic, legal, civic and political fields. The Heads of the College of Medical, Veterinary and Life Sciences and the College of Science and Engineering are both women. It has taken women 125 years to reach, and surpass, the 441 years of their exclusion. But what might the denied women have achieved in these 441 years?

Of course, these eventual positive developments have affected women powerfully; not only in the ability of many women in Scotland to attain high positions in public life, but in the employment and economic opportunities that they opened up for women in every section of society, and in their own agency in improving their lives. It's now more possible than it has ever been for girls and women in Scotland not only to count their blessings but to read and write them also.

But these are blessings denied to many, and to women in particular. Two-thirds of the world's 776 million illiterate adults are women. 130 million girls are not in school. I can read because the country I live in has prioritised free education equally for all, girls included.

Imagine two babies, twins, male and female, but otherwise born exactly the same – except they are treated and will act differently. According to global statistics, the results of this are that:

- *One will be registered at birth, the other won't.*

- *One will carry out only a third of the world's work hours, but will get 90% of the world's income for it.*

- *The other will carry out 75% of agricultural work, but own only 1% of the land.*

- *One will have a 5-times better chance than the other of becoming a member of parliament.*

- *One will start a war; the other will have only a 2% chance of signing a peace treaty to stop it.*[3]

Education and literacy are key indicators of access in many more aspects of life: employment, health, citizenship, political engagement. Women spend a greater percentage of their income on children's education and health than men do, so investment in their education benefits the coming generations as well. It's obviously been important in my own history, with a dozen teachers in my immediate family; in primary, secondary and tertiary education, in arts teaching and in teaching English as a foreign language.

My great-grandmother, Eliza Fleming Orr, daughter of the landscape gardener John Fleming, born in 1841, is recorded in the censuses of 1861 and 1871 as being a schoolteacher in Cardross, until she married James Orr in 1871. This would have been the village school, and any training she had was presumably on the job. Nevertheless, in family pictures, she looks to me like an archetypal Victorian schoolteacher – formidable, firm but also quite kindly.

But the first recorded teacher in the family was born in the 18th century. Archibald Gilchrist, my great-great-great-grandfather, was born the eldest son of a weaver in 1789, in the parish of Kildalton, Islay. Between 1815 and the time of his death in 1859, he was the parochial schoolmaster (and at various times also deputy postmaster and registrar) in the neighbouring parish of Kilchoman.

Mr Cameron and Mr McLeish

In the New Statistical Account of Scotland in 1845, the author of the entry for the parish of Kilchoman, Rev. Alex Cameron, minister of the parish, describes the parochial school as *'very inefficiently taught'*, and notes about the other schools in the parish (one supported by the Society for Propagating Christian Knowledge, one by the Edinburgh Gaelic School Society, and six independent ventures) that *'the branches taught are of the most ordinary description. None of*

Eliza Fleming Orr, 1896

the teachers received a classical education.'[4] Not exactly a ringing endorsement.

However, I am inclined to approach Mr Cameron's comments with some caution. His disapproval was not confined to educational provision in his parish. It extended to almost everything, not least his parishioners. Of their domestic lives, he declared:

> *'In their personal and domestic habits, the people are not cleanly.*
> *In many instances, the cattle occupy the same apartment with the*
> *family; and though fond of dress, and of appearing well-attired*
> *when they go abroad, at home they are slovenly. Their ordinary*
> *food is potatoes, with milk and fish. During a great part of the*
> *year, very little oatmeal is consumed. In their culinary arrange-*
> *ments, there is great want of economy. They are improvident in*
> *the use of their food, and wasteful of their clothing.'*

He was even more scathing about their character:

> *'As a people, they are shrewd, fond of gossip and story-telling;*
> *there is among them a strong bias to cunning and a want of truth-*
> *fulness. Of the grown-up population, the majority are unable to*
> *read; – their minds are, therefore, comparatively uninformed –*
> *and it cannot be said that they are either a moral, or a religious*
> *people; and from the influence which their confirmed habits are*
> *producing on the rising generation, who are receiving a moral and*
> *religious education, a very immediate and decided change is*
> *scarcely to be expected.'*

Much of this he attributes to the recent prevalence of *'illicit distilla-*
tion', which was universal: *'this led to the neglect of field labour, and*
to the destruction of the social virtues'.

But the author of the entry for the parish of Kilchoman in the
Old Statistical Account, published in 1794, paints a rather different
picture. Rev. John McLeish, the parish minister, writes of the character and manners of his parishioners:

> *'No objection can be made against their natural parts and abili-*
> *ties, which are subtle and ingenious. They are fond of their own*
> *country, and not much given to enlisting in the army or the navy.*
> *They marry young, and are greatly connected by intermarriages,*

which must always be the case with insular situations; and yet they are very kind to all strangers who come to reside among them, or visit them. They are in general as contented with their situation as most people, as they have the comforts and conveniences of life in a reasonable degree. The Gaelic is the language of the common people; yet English is pretty well understood, and taught in all our schools. The dance and the song, with shinty and putting the stone, are their chief amusements. Numbers of them play well on the violin and bagpipe. They have a natural ease and gracefulness of motion in the dance, which is peculiar to themselves. The gentlemen, once a year, treat the ladies with a ball, where cheerfulness and propriety of conduct, always preside, and more elegance of manners are to be seen, than could well be expected in so remote a situation.'[5]

This is not the only difference in the two accounts. Mr McLeish identifies himself with his parish to a much greater extent; he speaks of 'we' and 'our people' continuously. For Mr Cameron, it is always 'they' whom he refers to. Perhaps this is a linguistic matter. Mr McLeish takes pride in the fact that he preaches in both Gaelic and English. Mr Cameron is more dismissive of the islanders' native tongue: *'Gaelic is the language universally spoken by the natives in their intercourse with one another. The English language is very generally understood; and from the number of families and individuals from the low country settled in the island, it is much spoken. In proportion as the natives are becoming more enlightened by education, the Gaelic is definitely losing ground.'* One feels that Mr Cameron is probably not a native.

But their most noticeable divergence is on the question of economics. More than the undoubted personal differences between the two writers, these two reports, made less than fifty years apart, record the huge changes that took place in the agricultural practices and way of life on Islay during that time.

At the end of the 18th century, Islay was still predominantly a place of subsistence farming and fishing. On the arable coastland, crops of corn, barley, oats and potatoes were raised; the poor of the island lived on potatoes and fish for three-quarters of the year. The other principal crop raised was flax, which provided the main industry when woven into linen, with many islanders not only producing linen for their own use, and for rental income, but working all year round as weavers for the gentry. My great-great-great-great-grandfather, Peter Gilchrist, born in 1764, was a weaver.

Flax cultivation had been introduced and encouraged by a series of innovative and enlightened members of the Campbell clan, the Campbells of Shawfield, who were the owners of Islay for 120 years (having bought out another branch of the clan whose ownership, marked by indebtedness and absenteeism, had been much less successful, both for them and for the people of Islay). The Shawfield Campbells also encouraged a nascent fishing industry, built roads, introduced a ferry service to the mainland which carried the mail, and established schools. Even the people's health was improved when the whole island was inoculated against smallpox, and Mr McLeish reports that the poor were inoculated free of charge.

Improvements also extended to agriculture. Islay, like almost everywhere else in Scotland, operated the feudal system of land ownership. The island's patron was the king, for which privilege he extracted 500 hundred Scots Pounds each year (a huge sum then; the minister's annual stipend was only 50 Scots Pounds). Mr Campbell of Shawfield owned the whole island, but leased some of it to what were known as tacksmen, who were large tenants and ranked among the gentry. Much of their energy on Islay seems to have been devoted to breeding black cattle, which at this time commanded high prices. The tacksmen in turn employed the ordinary people to work on their farms. Small tenants lived together in towns or townships, comprising an area of cultivable land and a larger area of common pasture and rough grazing, in a way of farming long practised throughout the Highlands and known as 'run rig'.

Mr McLeish considered Mr Campbell to be an exemplary proprietor, who had given his tenants such advantageous leases that they had been able to greatly improve their standard of living (as well as double the rents they paid him). Mostly this seems to have been achieved by bringing many acres of moorland into arable cultivation. These improvements meant that very few of the tenants chose to emigrate. Plenty of peat and fish-oil available for heat and light, *'make the habitation of the meanest cottager warm and cheery'*.

But the minister ends his report on the improvements with a cautionary word:

> *'When tenants are emancipated from the avarice of monopolisers, they seem to breathe a purer air, and improvements go on rapidly; for nothing has tended more to excite the spirit of emigration, than the Demon of Monopoly, which leads the avaricious to add land to land and farm to farm. The writer of this article cannot approve of the maxim "That the more rents you lay on, the tenants will work the better." This, like the Egyptian bondage, is exacting bricks without straw, and tends to check, rather than incite, the spirit of industry. But if the moderation and lenity [gentleness], that have hitherto been observed in Islay, continue to be adhered to, we may venture to promise, that the people may rather stay at home, to improve the lands of their native island, rather than go abroad to cultivate the wilds of America. Amen!'*

How times change. The population of Islay, which had been around 5300 in 1755, increased to over 8000 by 1802, and by 1831, the island had 15,000 inhabitants. In part, this was the result of better times in the latter half of the 18th century. Increased food security, defence against smallpox, and the increased income from fishing, kelp production, linen manufacture and distilling had all led to fewer untimely deaths and an increased birth rate. But this population level was unsustainable; there was huge pressure on land, the good prices for cattle and crops fell after the end of the Napoleonic Wars, which also saw the collapse of the kelp industry, and the greater mechanisation of weaving, along with competition from flax imported from the Baltic, had more or less destroyed the weaving industry. The tacksmen who had held large tenancies and enjoyed considerable influence were now, according to Mr Cameron, nearly extinct. This fact he attributes to their previous affluence: *'their prosperity became the cause of their ruin'*. Having adopted the style of life of landed proprietors, when the markets fell and their incomes declined, they did not tighten their belts accordingly, and had to make way for tenants *'of more economical habits'*.

Among the poorer parts of the population, many people were now unable to pay their rent. Mr Campbell of Shawfield, the current proprietor (and grandson of the previous exemplary owner), being a humane man, did not wish to encourage mass emigration, and encouraged the people to move to villages which he had constructed. But the spread of potato blight from Ireland in the mid-1840s was the final blow in this period of decline. This impacted not only on the quality of cattle that small tenants kept (affecting the quantity and quality of their fodder), with falling prices meaning they had to sell off their best stock to meet rising rents. Thousands of people now faced the real danger of starvation, and the trickle of emigrants grew to a flood. It was around this time that my great-great-grandmother, Marrion Gilchrist, left Islay for Glasgow.

Mr Cameron devotes much of his account to describing the changes taking place in farming practices: the draining, ditching and enclosure of very wet, boggy land, though he comments that compared to what still might be done, such improvements are only in their infancy. He attributes the slow pace of change to two principal factors. The first is the continuing prevalence of the run rig system, grazing the pasture land in common. Mr Cameron has a very low opinion of this traditional system, which he sees as standing in the way of the amalgamation of small holdings into much larger and more profitable sheep farms. His theology is not critical, as Mr McLeish's was, of the Demon of Monopoly. He writes: '*The obstacles which this mode of holding land presents to persons of skill and industry, in clearing and improving their lands, need not be detailed here; – to say that the system obtains is enough to suggest them to every enlightened, and intelligent mind.*'

Nor is Mr Cameron sympathetic to those who might suffer under the '*Egyptian bondage*'. The other factor standing in the way of progress, as Mr Cameron sees it, is the general and almost universal practical and moral failings of the people themselves, as exemplified by their lack of skill in availing themselves of the opportunities offered by drainage, their bad management of sheep as a profitable enterprise, and by their failure to fish for the markets (limiting their fishing to feeding their own families). '*Being partly fishers and partly agriculturalists, they pursue neither vocation with proper energy.*' He feels that '*on the whole, there is great lack of capital, industry and enterprise among them*', though the conditions of farm leases are decidedly favourable to those '*who know the value of land, and are in possession of capital and enterprise*'. Mr Cameron seems to view the lack of capital as a character flaw. Most damning of all, '*a dislike to continuous labour prevails extensively among the working-classes*'.

Curiously, this moral turpitude does not seem to inhibit the people from displaying another characteristic usually thought of as being among the higher Christian virtues, that of love of neighbour. '*A feeling of independence still obtains, and it is considered a degradation to have one's relatives partially supported by the parish. The wants of the poor are frequently supplied by neighbours. The parish finds bedding when necessary; food and fuel are easily procured, and it is rarely any house-rent is exacted.*' It is not clear whether Mr Cameron approves of this feeling of independence.

Both Mr Cameron's description of the land changes taking place, and his opinion of the people's fecklessness, are a vivid and precise demonstration of the deeper ideological and economic shift that was already well under way across the Highlands of Scotland, which was about to intensify considerably in Islay. Land which had formerly been used primarily for subsistence farming, with cattle as a secondary source of income, was increasingly seen as an asset, and a source of profit. Sheep farming was seen to offer the highest returns, but could only do so if done on a large scale. This in turn required a big reduction in the number of small tenancies, which were then consolidated into much larger ones, for which higher rents could be charged. The enclosure of the common grazing land by landowners, ending a community practice which had existed for centuries, added more land to the large farms – but it had an additional purpose. Small tenants who found themselves displaced, and moved to coastal villages and crofting townships, now found that they did not have enough land to survive and feed their families. They would therefore be obliged to become waged labourers, taking seasonal employment on the large farms or on fishing boats. They would no longer have the status of tenant farmers.

Since it was now important to have a biddable and hardworking itinerant labour force, and since a dispossessed and resentful population who had been accustomed to work to live were not the most reliable prospect, a way had to be found to persuade them that they now needed to live to work. How to do this was a question which greatly exercised Mr Cameron. He has already commented on their dislike to continuous labour, and asks: *'How is this to be changed? As their natural wants do not seem to be sufficiently stimulating to produce a change, a more efficient moral influence, by means of the force of education on the female mind, must be brought to bear on the general character.'*

I must say, I was not expecting that. But Mr Cameron elaborates. He has informed his readers that while all the young people are taught to read, only the boys are taught to write and figure. Now he offers his rationale for the importance of education for girls. *'As the feelings and habits of the young are necessarily formed to a great degree by females, it is reasonable to suppose that the impressions which they communicate, modify the character of the future man. When their mind is so totally unenlightened with the knowledge of Divine things, they cannot convey correct ideas of moral obligation, or of relative duties, or of the place which personal labour holds in the scheme of God's moral government. Idly disposed, and exhibiting a conduct governed by prej-udices handed down from past generations, they not only do not con-tribute to the means of supporting the family, but they do not use judiciously or economically what is committed to their trust, nor easily adopt the suggestions of persons who are better informed. It is antici-pated, that, as these habits and feelings give way to the force of Scrip-tural education, the comfort, morals and happiness of the labouring classes will be promoted.'*

Indeed, I do not find it difficult to dislike Mr Cameron. His instinct about the importance of educating girls does not seem to be at all for its own merits, or for their well-being. This is a scheme for the inculcation of a Protestant work ethic to serve the interests of the capitalist classes, premised on the moral inferiority of the labouring classes who dare to ignore the advice of their betters, all wrapped up in the myth of progress and given the dubious authori-sation of claiming to know God's views on moral government. He has none of Mr McLeish's warm appreciation of the culture, kind-ness and hospitality of the Islay people, nor any discernable pastoral care for them. I wonder how he and Archibald Gilchrist, my ineffi-cient schoolmaster great-great-great-grandfather, got on.

Over the next few decades, thousands emigrated from Islay, mostly to Canada. The Campbells of Shawfield, who had run up huge debts, at least in part through their improvement programmes, went into bankruptcy, and Islay was sold off in 1853. The estates were eventually broken up and sold on to private individuals, and so it remains today, with much of Islay owned by a few private owners, some of them absentee, some of them hidden behind private trusts and companies. Its population at the 2011 census was 3228, and farming, fishing and tourism all go on. But the backbone of the island's economy, for which it is famous worldwide, is distilling. The most recent distillery to be built is in Mr Cameron's former parish.

Notes:

1. Kathy Galloway, in *A Scottish Childhood, Volume II*, compiled by Nancy E M Bailey, Harper Collins Publishers, 1998

2. Lindy Moore, from 'Education and Learning' in *Gender in Scottish History since 1700*, ed. Lynn Abrams, Eleanor Gordon, Deborah Simonton and Eileen Janes Yeo, Edinburgh University Press, 2006; and A. Bain, *Patterns of Error: The Teacher and External Authority in Central Scotland, 1581-1861*, Mowbray House Publishing, 1989, p.26. Reproduced with permission of the Licensor through PLSclear

3. From Christian Aid

4. Quotes from Rev. Alex Cameron from New Statistical Account of Scotland in 1845, Kilchoman, County of Argyle, NSA Vol. VII, 1845

5. Quotes from Rev. John McLeish from Old Statistical Account, Kilchoman, County of Argyle, OSA Vol. XI, 1794

Migration and empire, 1829-2020

The first time I left the shores of Scotland, I was 22 years old, and to go 'abroad' was a great adventure for someone for whom travel had hitherto meant childhood holidays spent in Fife, Helensburgh and Iona and a couple of cross-border ventures to visit relatives living in England. The reality of 'abroad' actually included having to push an elderly and overloaded Vauxhall Viva off the Dover to Ostend ferry, driving rather slowly in the direction of Bruges, and then, with night having fallen, pitching a tent in complete darkness in what we thought was a campsite, but which morning revealed to be a field only separated by a hedge from the motorway. And though I have remained ambivalent about camping ever since, the charm of the quiet canals of Bruges, and the excitement of eating baguettes and pommes frites with mayonnaise, which were so *foreign* compared to Scottish sliced white bread and chips with nippy sauce, summed up the delight of being 'abroad' for me for many years.

Since that time, I have travelled extensively in every continent except Antarctica, mostly for work. I have enjoyed a degree of mobility almost unimaginable for anyone born before the middle of the 20th century. And though some of my travel has been demanding and occasionally quite difficult, I have never lost a sense of anticipation about being 'abroad', nor a sense of privilege at the opportunity it has given me to experience just a little of the extraordinary diversity and beauty of the world and its peoples.

The migrants who came

And yet, as I explore the lives of my forebears, I see that mobility and migration marked some of their lives also, and that some of them made very long and life-changing journeys, not always by choice. Our family research only goes back, at most, about 350 years – a relatively short time – and as far as we know, the period from the late 17th century until almost the middle of the 19th century was marked by the fact that there is no record of any inward migration into Scotland. During that period, almost every single person in my direct ancestry was Scottish. There are three exceptions to this. My great-great-great-great-grandmother, born in 1764 and married to the Islay weaver Peter Gilchrist, was Catherine Connely; another four times great grandfather was John Laverty, a labourer in Ayrshire. Both of these are common Irish names; Catherine may have been an Irish weaver looking to use her skills in the developing Islay linen industry and John's family part of the constant stream of coming and going between west coast Scotland and Ireland, particularly Ulster, which is so very close. And Michael Lamond, my great-great-great grandfather, father of the West Lothian shale miner, was also born in Ireland.

Speculative reaching further back would also suggest a Low Countries connection in the name Fleming; many immigrants from Flanders settled in south Scotland. And like many Scottish families, ours also, on my mother's side, has a story of a Spanish ancestor in a sailor from the Armada in the 16th century (mostly, as far as we can tell, told in order to account for the striking dark colouring of some of the family). There is no evidence for any of these stories, but any origin for this myth could only have come from Islay, where among the hundreds of shipwrecks around the coasts might have been one from the Armada.

We are on much firmer ground with the Irish ancestor we can be sure of, my great-great-grandfather, Maurice Morrin, born in Ireland in 1829, the son of Patrick Morrin and Alison Gribbon, and by the mid-19th century living in the West of Scotland. We assume he migrated, as so many did, as a result of the famine. When I was perhaps eleven or twelve, I learned in school about the Great Famine in 19th-century Ireland. This was in a Scottish context; an explanation of why so many Irish people had immigrated into the West of Scotland, with far-reaching consequences for a very predominantly Protestant country. I learned about the hostility of many of the native population to these economic migrants, who they accused of pushing down wages (being so desperate, they would work for very low rates), or simply of taking their jobs. I learned about the sectarian religious conflicts that arose between Scottish Protestants and Irish Catholics, and which, in tribal forms, still persist today as a scar upon Scotland. I learned about the horrors of the famine itself, of children eating grass, of families dying in ditches, and was left in no doubt about its catastrophic nature. About a million people died of starvation or epidemic diseases between 1846-1851; another two million emigrated in little more than a decade. The retelling of this tragic story in 1960s Edinburgh was by no means unsympathetic.

But I was not taught that during all the years of the famine, grain was being both exported and imported in large quantities, and that, from 1847, there was enough food in Ireland to prevent this mass starvation if only it had been properly distributed. What began as a natural disaster caused by potato blight, very soon became an artificial famine. But Ireland was at this time not an independent nation, it was ruled by a British government, part of what was then the richest country in the world. Why did the government not do more to alleviate the plight of its own subjects? There was no war in the country, a reasonable infrastructure of roads and canals, no great distances to traverse, a strong bureaucracy of civil servants – all difficulties prevalent in contemporary famines.

There were ideological factors which prevented the British political elite and middle classes from taking the kind of relief actions that were perfectly possible. The first was economic. The new Whig government, led by Lord John Russell, espoused the economic orthodoxy of the day in their laissez-faire belief that the market would provide and there should be as little government interference as possible. To stop the food exports, they believed, would be an unacceptable policy alternative. They then halted government food and relief works, leaving hundreds of thousands without work, money or food.

The second factor was to be found in the Protestant evangelical belief in divine Providence. There was a widespread belief among the British middle and upper-middle classes that the famine was a divine judgement against the inefficient and corrupt Irish agricultural system. Since the hand of God was perceived to be revealed in the unfettered workings of the market economy, it was considered positively evil to interfere with its proper functioning. Sir Charles Trevelyan, the British civil servant who was in charge of the administration of government relief to the victims of the Irish Famine, limited the Government's actual relief because, he proclaimed, *'the judgment of God sent the calamity to teach the Irish a lesson'* and he described the famine as *'a direct stroke of an all-wise and all-merciful providence'.*[1] The fact that the Irish agricultural system had largely evolved as a result of deeply unjust land laws and denial of tenant rights was loftily overlooked. And this attribution to God of what was very evidently in the interest of British policy-makers allowed the mass evictions that led to the radical restructuring of Irish rural society into the more preferred capitalistic model.

The third factor in the failure of Britain to prevent a million of its subjects starving to death was what has come to be known as 'moralism'. This deep-dyed and well-documented ethnic prejudice and cultural stereotyping had the general effect of prompting British ministers, civil servants, and politicians to view and to treat the Catholic Irish as something less than fully human.

The Irish historian Jim Donnelly writes:

'Such prejudices encouraged the spread of "famine fatigue" in Britain at an early stage, and they dulled or even extinguished the active sympathies that might have sustained political will – the will to combat the gross oppression of mass evictions, to alleviate the immense suffering associated with reliance on the poor-law system, and to grapple with the moral indefensibility of mass death in the midst of an absolute sufficiency of food.'[2]

In 19th-century Ireland, food was a weapon and tool of control. It is not hard to see in these very prevalent attitudes and practices the same ideology (and it is an ideology) that prompted our old friend Mr Cameron in his dismissive comments on the people of his Islay parish in the New Statistical Account. Dirty, lazy, cunning, untruthful, profligate, drunk and disorderly – the accusations are the same, and so is the moralising and the unwavering conviction of rectitude, righteousness and a hotline to the Almighty. The Irish poor were mostly Catholic, and the Islay poor were Protestant; it is not hard to read behind these religious differences to the real motive in the prejudicial stereotyping of the Gaelic culture of both communities – forced evictions and emigration, and the enclosure of the commons in the interests of capitalistic landowners. Maurice Morrin from Ireland and Marrion Gilchrist from Islay must have found they already had much which united them when they met and married in the mainland West of Scotland.

Other than this Gaelic wedding, all the branches of our family continued until the middle of the 20th century to do what they had always done; that is, they married people who lived in the same part of the country, or even in the same parish. When they moved, it was usually only a few miles – to a neighbouring farm, as with the Ayrshire Campbells; to a new pit when an old seam was exhausted for the mining Thomsons and Johnstons in Stirlingshire and West Lothian; to a new shop for the Glasgow Orrs.

The migrants who went

– to the plantations of the Caribbean

But if inward migration was limited, things were very different when it came to outward migration. In 1843, Robert Christie died at the age of 17 in the Caribbean island of Tobago. Robert was the half-brother of my great-grandfather Henry Campbell, though he died when Henry was only two years old. Their mother, Marion Farquhar, had lost her first husband when they were both in their twenties.

She had then married the young widower John Campbell, and together they had raised her two children from her first marriage, and their own eleven children. But what was a teenage boy, son of an exciseman and stepson of a farmer, doing in Tobago?

There isn't a good answer to this question, because it probably relates to the sorry involvement of Scotland in general, and Glasgow in particular, in slavery in the Caribbean. Though the port of Glasgow, and its nearby satellite ports of Greenock and Port Glasgow, had relatively little involvement in the actual trading of slaves to the Americas in comparison to other British ports such as Liverpool and Bristol, it was heavily engaged in the trading of commodities produced in the American plantations, particularly those of the Caribbean. Cotton, sugar and tobacco were traded in vast amounts through Scotland (mostly Glasgow), at times more than all the English ports combined. Many merchants grew hugely rich through this trade; this is how the so-called Tobacco Lords got their wealth. Glasgow prospered as a mercantile city with tobacco from the Virginias and sugar from the Caribbean, produced by the labour of black chattel slaves.

But it wasn't just the trading. It was also about the role of Scots as owners, managers and overseers of the plantations themselves. In Jamaica, it is estimated that around one-third of plantations were Scots-owned, and since many of the wealthy Scots owners had no wish to actually live there, job opportunities opened up for their relatives, employees and other young Scotsmen, as managers and overseers. Thousands of them travelled to the Caribbean slave islands in the second half of the 18th century, including to Tobago, where Scots largely ran the plantations. The oppression and cruelty of plantation life, and the brutality of the overseers and managers, has been well-documented, and is well-known, though it is too easily forgotten, and little known at all by Scots, who are over-inclined to paint ourselves as victims of oppression.

The British slave trade was ended in 1807. But the trading of plantation products – cotton, indigo, rum and particularly sugar – continued, and in fact increased. The emancipation of slaves did not happen in Tobago until 1834, and even then, a system of bonded labour, lasting around five years, was supposed to make the transition easier – for the owners. 11,589 slaves were freed, and compensation of £233,875 (an enormous amount, equivalent to many millions today) was paid – to the owners. At this time, the majority of the white population of Tobago was Scottish. After the unconditional ending of slavery in 1838, unsurprisingly, many of the former slaves left the land, and a labour shortage ensued. A metayage system, a form of share-cropping formerly common in France and in French colonies, developed from 1843 onwards, and was the main means of sugar production until the end of the 19th century, when sugar production was finally abandoned. The register of merchant seamen includes Robert Christie; as the son of an exciseman in Greenock, one of the main ports trading with the Caribbean. It seems that Tobago was where he died on one of these trading voyages.

There is nothing about this story which is not sad. To die at 17, so far from home and family, is an individual tragedy. The shocking silence in Scotland about our complicity with and profit from slavery in all its aspects (this is another part of Scottish history which we were not taught about at school) has been shameful. Some years ago, I got to know a little the distinguished poet and lawyer M. NourbeSe Philip, who was born and raised in Tobago, though she now lives in Canada. Drinking coffee on a sunny day in Toronto, we spoke about our families, and she recalled her grandfather, who, it transpired, had a very Scottish surname.

In her extraordinary, award-winning sequence of poems, *She Tries Her Tongue; Her Silence Softly Breaks*, Philip wrestles with the problem of recollecting the self in the present, of re-membering when that crucial member the tongue, the word, is absent or inaccessible or poisoned.

Edict I

Every owner of slaves shall, wherever possible, ensure that his slaves belong to as many ethno-linguistic groups as possible. If they cannot speak to each other, they cannot then foment rebellion and revolution.

Edict II

Every slave caught speaking his native language shall be severely punished. Where necessary, removal of the tongue is recommended. The offending organ, when removed, should be hung on high in a central place, so that all may see and tremble.

> *when the smallest cell remembers —*
> *how do you*
> *how can you*
> *when the smallest cell*
>   *remembers*
> *lose a language*
>
> *absencelosstears laughter   grief*
> *in any language*
>   *the same*
> *only larger*
>   *for the silence*
>   *monstrosity*
> *obscenity*
> *tongueless wonder*
> *blackened stump of a tongue*
>   *torn*
> *out*
>   *withered*
>   *petrified*
>   *burnt*

on the pyres of silence
a mother's child foreign
                              made
by a tongue that cursed
                    the absence
in loss
tears   laughtergrief
                    in the word

 Hold we to the centre of remembrance
   that forgets the never that severs
         word from source
   and never forgets the witness
   of broken utterances that passed
         before   and now
     breaks the culture of silence
     in the ordeal of testimony;
     in the history of circles
         each point lies
     along the circumference
         diameter or radius
     each word creates a centre
circumscribed by memory ... and history
         waits   at rest always

     still at the centre[3]

Robert Christie was only the first of a long line of emigrants in my family.

– to the coal mines of America

In 1847, my great-great-great-grandparents James Miller and Elizabeth Brownlie, along with six of their seven children, embarked in Glasgow on the *Ann Harley*, bound for New York. The seventh child, Ann, alone of her family, remained in Scotland, in the gardener's lodge at Kilmahew Castle. The Millers travelled steerage, the lowest cost, lowest class of travel, where conditions were appalling and overcrowded, often accommodating hundreds in large cargo spaces below decks, food was dreadful and fresh water and fresh air were both in short supply. This was how millions of poor emigrants from Europe crossed the Atlantic. They moved to West Virginia, a coal mining state, where James could find work in his old occupation; Ann's brother John died in Lancaster County, Pennsylvania, in 1908.

In 1906, my great-uncle Andrew Thomson emigrated to Canton, Illinois, where he worked as a coal miner. 20 years later, he returned to Scotland and worked as a colliery under-manager at Loganlea Colliery.

In 1911, my great-uncle Alexander Thomson emigrated to Philadelphia, worked as a coal miner in Northern Pennsylvania, and died in Detroit, where he worked for Ford Motors, in 1948.

– to the colonies

In 1861, my great-great-great-uncle, Henry Campbell, farmer by profession, died on board ship during a passage to Australia at the age of 52.

In 1902, my great-uncle John Fleming Orr emigrated to South Africa, and lived there for the rest of his life, working as a chartered accountant and building society manager in Cape Town and Johannesburg. He returned to Scotland several times, not travelling steerage.

In 1903, my great-uncle James Fleming Gordon Orr migrated to New Zealand. James Orr was a missionary, a somewhat ambivalent term today. His first 'foreign field' was not exactly on the frontline of evangelisation; he was teaching and examining Hebrew and Greek in the Otago region of the South Island of New Zealand. It had been settled in the mid-19th century by Scottish Presbyterians, and teaching biblical languages in a Presbyterian theological college in such a strongly Scottish-influenced place was probably not so different from doing it in Glasgow.

His next missionary assignment was very different. In March 1921, he and Grace, his wife, sailed to Mombasa in Kenya, to take up an appointment in Nairobi, on behalf of the Colonial Committee of the Church of Scotland. The *Dundee Courier and Advertiser* carried an interview with him in September 1929, as a former local minister. It's titled 'Advance of Kenya Colony: Where Natives Are Fond of Football'. He is described as the Church of Scotland Chaplain in the colony, headquartered in Nairobi, and his first words in the article set the tone. *'It is roughly 30 years since the pioneers entered Kenya. And within that short time, it is wonderful what civilisation has done for the natives.'*[4] He describes the terrain of Kenya, and recommends the highlands, lying between 6000 and 8000 feet high, inland from Nairobi, as the ideal spot for settlers. However, he sounds a note of warning: no one should ever think of taking up farming in Kenya unless he has sufficient capital behind him; in fact, nothing less than £3000 would give him security. Many young fellows who had taken up farming there had failed, not because of themselves, but because they did not have sufficient money to carry them through a bad season. He goes on to describe the crops grown, the recent dry season and plagues of locusts, the strenuous fight against tropical maladies and the drainage of swampy regions.

The next section of the article is headed 'Clever Natives'. The population of Nairobi consists of 4000 Europeans, 10,000 Indians and 30,000 African natives, most of whom belong to the Kikuyu tribe. James says that the Wa Kikuyu have proved themselves very clever, and are working along the Europeans in workshops. They take a great pride in themselves, are always keen to learn, and like to be smartly dressed. They trusted the white man, and would always stand by him.

We then come to a point of particular familial interest: *'no one enjoys a game of football more than the natives. They are great footballers, and play with their bare feet. I have seen a man kick the ball nearly the whole length of the field. They love sport, and they enter into it with the proper spirit.'*[5]

James next seeks to *'clear up a misunderstanding which seems to be quite prevalent at home, and which concerns the treatment of the natives. I can say with all truth that the treatment of the natives by the whites is exemplary. If any man is found guilty of cruelty or bad treatment of a native, there are no people more down on him than his fellow settlers.'*[6] This, at a time when the creation of the white-settler-dominated Kenya Crown Colony was giving rise to considerable political activity against colonial injustices, land occupation and appropriation, and Jomo Kenyatta was being sent to London to air Kikuyu grievances against British occupation and rule.

On he goes. Superstition and witchcraft have been definitely left far behind, and the native appreciates civilisation, and what it can do for him. But – and it is quite a 'but' – all of this applies only to the men. The native women refuse to show any initiative, and do not appreciate the benefits of civilisation. *'We have the greatest difficulty in getting these women to give up the old customs, even although some of them be harmful and hurtful.'*[7] James is of the opinion that the backwardness of the women would in a very short time lead to an acute problem, because the men are advancing rapidly along modern lines, and they will naturally not like to take ignorant women as wives.

The missions and their hospitals are accomplishing fine work in the colony on behalf of the natives, and the Government is now realising the indispensable aid it is receiving in opening up the country. He notes the feeling in some quarters that, now the country is being opened up, the white folk should leave the colony, but the native would rather have the whites beside him than be left alone with the Indians. His final word is that this is a young country with great possibilities.

The effortless assumption of white superiority and what we would now consider to be explicit racism are striking, though clearly not in 1929. James is defending the colonial project, and the settler interests, to the hilt, seeing them as a vital context for his 'civilising', and probably quite benevolently intended, mission. From other accounts, we know that his own grievances against Britain concerned the failure of the Crown to properly respect the status of the Church of Scotland in Kenya – he was most upset that formal occasions involving the ordinances of religion were given to the Anglicans. He was always a great defender of the equal importance of Scots in and to the British Empire. He remained in Kenya for the rest of his life, becoming the first minister of St Andrews Church of Scotland in Nairobi, now part of the Presbyterian Church of East Africa since 1956, and with the first Kenyan Senior Pastor installed in 1975. Today, St Andrews is a flourishing church with over 4000 members.

In 1912, my great-uncle Harry Campbell emigrated to Canada and worked as a butcher in Vancouver.

In 1918, to Ghana (then the Gold Coast), Thomas Imrie, husband of my great-aunt Margaret Campbell.

In 1926, to Buenos Aires, my second cousin Alexandra Campbell Todd.

In 1926, my great-uncle Adam Campbell emigrated to Australia, and lived in Australia and New Zealand, working as a salesman till his death in 1949.

In 1930, to India, my second cousin Margaret Paterson Todd, where her husband Ron Mackay was a tea planter.

In 1953, my aunt, Agnes Johnston, the sister closest to my mother in age, and throughout their lives, moved to Geneva,

James Fleming Gordon Orr, 1910

Switzerland. Unable to stay on at school, she had trained in short-hand and typing at night school, and got a job as a secretary at the International Labour Organisation (ILO). There she learned to ski, and made many friends. My mother's first holiday abroad was a visit with our father to stay with her in Geneva.

Around 1960, Agnes moved with her husband Bill Cluness to Nigeria, where he had an appointment via the Church of Scotland's Overseas Council (the successor to the Colonial Committee) to work as the General Manager of a leprosy hospital in Itu, then to a similar post at the Presbyterian Joint Hospital in Uburu, Ebonyi. Both Itu and Uburu are in south-eastern Nigeria, and were part of the territory that seceded from Nigeria in 1967 as the Republic of Biafra. In the brutal civil war that followed, almost a million Biafran civilians (most of them small children) died from starvation or disease caused by the total blockade of the region by the Nigerian government. Agnes and her two small children were recalled to Scotland by the Overseas Council; Bill remained in Biafra, and became involved with colleagues in the dangerous business of breaking the blockade to run food supplies to starving people. He, an engineer by profession, also found himself acting as an anaesthetist for emergency surgery being performed under war conditions.

For two years, I babysat once a week for Agnes, who was living in a flat in Edinburgh with the children. I would have an evening meal with them, then look after the children and put them to bed, while Agnes caught up with friends, family and other Nigeria colleagues. I would stay overnight and go to school from there in the morning. In the evening, after Agnes returned, we would sit for a while talking about the war, about the limited news she was receiving from Bill, and about Biafra. I learned that the British colonial policy that divided Nigeria into three regions – North, West and East – had exacerbated the already well-developed economic, political, and social differences among Nigeria's different ethnic groups, and helped to sow the seeds that led to the secession and the war. She was an admirer of its young leader, Colonel Odumegwu Ojukwu, and was extremely critical of the UK Government's position, in support of the Federal Government, but really quite blatantly in support only of its oil interests and companies. In 1967, 30% of the oil being imported into Britain came from Nigeria. The war, and the increasingly dire plight of the Biafrans, became an international scandal.

Its end came in early 1970, with the surrender of Biafra, and Bill finally came home. Having been on the wrong side, so to speak, the Nigerian authorities would not grant them a visa to return to work in the country. Agnes went on to hold a senior administrative role with Edinburgh City Council. In later life, now widowed, she travelled several times alone to Turkey, where she made some deep friendships and learned to speak Turkish. And she learned to play the flute. She was a kind, spirited and adventurous woman, and these late-night conversations with her were the beginnings of my education on British colonialism.

In 1964, my uncle, Lyall Orr, emigrated with his wife and three daughters to St Andrews, New Brunswick, Canada.

In 1962, my cousin Sylvia Douglas emigrated to Durban, South Africa.

In 1964, my cousin Lesley Orr emigrated to Toronto, Canada.

In 1973, my cousin Marian Orr emigrated to Tokyo, Japan.

– to the world

In the generation following my own, within our immediate and extended family, our young have migrated, temporarily or permanently, all over the world. Our family is an international one, and has been for more than a century. Globalisation is not new.

None of these individuals migrated as the result of political or religious persecution (though the Irish migrants came from a context of extreme political and religious discrimination). Nevertheless, their experience varied widely. The Millers in the 1840s and the Thomson brothers in the very early 20th century left the coal mines of Scotland for the coal mines of the United States, exchanging one set of grim living and working conditions for another, travelling as poor people, but hoping for new opportunities in the land of the free. The middle-class Campbells and Orrs, over a hundred-year period, took advantage of the British Empire to relocate to its colonies, mostly permanently, and generally speaking, flourished in their new homes.

And in my lifetime, from the mid-20th century onwards, the Scots from our family who have left Scotland have been able to do so really as a result of their white privilege, sometimes because they profited from the colonial legacy and could relocate with relative ease to Canada, Australia, New Zealand, South Africa; sometimes for study, or just for adventure, because they could. The most recent migrants could do it because the UK was a member of the European Union. We have no contact at all with the American migrants; but for over a hundred years, our family has maintained the close connection between Scotland and Canada, where members of the extended family are spread out from the Maritimes to British Columbia, and now include French Canadians. We come and go between Scotland and Canada regularly.

All of these people were, in one way or another, economic migrants. They, especially the earlier ones, made lengthy, sometimes squalid journeys to find a new and better life for themselves and their families. Public attitudes to the millions who went this way from Scotland over the last two hundred years are interesting. We think of them as brave, resourceful, heroic even. We are compassionate towards the plight that led them to leave – the clearances, poverty and destitution they suffered – and we sing songs and write poems about the pain of leaving the land and the ones they loved behind, and about the hardships they endured in the new world. And when their descendants return to the old country to visit, we rightly welcome them with open arms and praise their achievements and their prosperity; the towns and cities they founded, the businesses they built up, the churches they planted as they took their faith with them. We are proud of what they did.

How curious, then, that our attitudes to immigrants into Europe should be so different. Misunderstanding, racism, relentless hostility are daily experiences for many. To be part of a minority, especially a visibly or audibly different one, is to always have to prove one's belonging, and to have no signs of proof ever be enough. Previous generations of immigrants to and within Europe, attempting to belong, to assimilate, were met by a queasy mixture of racism and exploitation of their labour. Their second- and third-generation children, perhaps more confident, or more cynical, have called us on our professions of democracy and individual freedoms, and asserted an identity of difference. In this, they are doing what emigrating Europeans have always done, whether that be in the mission and church planting in Africa and South America which accompanied colonialism, or in expatriate enclaves, or in supplanting indigenous cultures altogether to become the unquestioned majority; they have carried their language, culture, religion, politics and economics, and, let us not forget, in some of these places, their military capacity with them, to create places where they could feel at home, where they could belong without always having to prove it. So many Scots have family members, in the recent or the long-ago past, who have been economic migrants, that it behoves us to treat the ones who come here with a degree of fellow-feeling, even empathy. They have been us; they are us; they will be us.

My family visits are a small part of the travelling I have done since that first European venture. Most of my sojourns in foreign lands have not been for holidays, but have been what could more accurately been described as solidarity visits. That is to say, they have been made with, and on behalf of, a wide range of church, interfaith and community organisations, women's groups, and international aid organisations. I have stayed mostly in hostels, colleges, church centres and a very large number of private homes.

I have visited forty countries in Europe, Africa, the Americas, Asia and Oceania, refugee camps in three continents and indigenous settlements in four. I have made two long tours in the USA visiting 21 states (travelling mostly by Greyhound Bus, by choice, in one of these), one in Canada visiting seven provinces, and one to every state in Australia. Such travel gave me a very interesting perspective on some aspects of being Scots-originated in these former colonies.

In 2000, at the invitation of the Presbyterian Church of the USA, the traditional denomination of choice of many Americans of Scottish descent, I spent six weeks as part of its International Peacemakers programme, visiting Kentucky, south-west Missouri and Kansas, San Francisco and the Bay area, West Jersey (taking in Atlantic City at one end and Philadelphia at the other), the endless skies of Nebraska ('our sky is like your sea') and Washington DC. I enjoyed great hospitality and courtesy almost everywhere, but it was a steep learning curve for me. In one Missouri town, I asked my host about its economic base. He replied that it was its hospitals. At that time, I genuinely did not understand his response; my post-war Scottish upbringing had given me no comprehension of healthcare as a free enterprise, for-profit business. His further description of the free clinics being run by some of the doctors from the hospitals, to which people too poor to afford health insurance travelled from four surrounding states to attend, gave me a new appreciation of the NHS, which continues to grow as it continues to be threatened by the same market ideology.

I discovered that in many parts of the USA, Presbyterians are considered dangerously radical (a novel experience for a Scot). One day, looking at the long food lines outside one (not wealthy) city church I found myself torn between profound respect for the sacrificial service involved in feeding all these people day after day, and the appalled thought: 'How are they not utterly ashamed that their country, the richest and most powerful on earth, relies on charity to feed its poor!' The Presbyterians, and other mainline traditions, were up against stiff competition – I saw the gospel of prosperity demonstrably practised in place of the gospel of Jesus Christ in white evangelical churches in the Bible Belt. In a Missouri Bible college, I was shocked to the core to have the suitability of my clothing assessed and to be asked by its male principal to remove my (tiny) nose stud; it seemed an insupportable thing to ask of a middle-aged guest from another country who was about to address a social anthropology class. I have never been so rudely treated anywhere else in the world. Often, the quality of food eaten by ordinary people was awful. I was asked everywhere about gun control, and my attempt on one occasion to explain the complete British banning of handguns in response to the Dunblane massacre met with baffled disbelief, only surpassed when I requested to walk places.

In New Jersey, I was asked if the Kirking of the Tartan was a big service in my home church. I had to confess that I had never heard of it anywhere in Scotland. The questioner seemed disappointed; it transpires that the service, which takes place all over North America, was initiated in the 1940s by a Presbyterian minister of Scots origin in New York, and is loosely based on some dubious mythology about the Jacobite Rising of 1745 (whose protagonists were primarily Catholic and Episcopalian). But it's really a celebration of Scottish heritage, along with the kilts, pipe bands, Scottish country dancing, Highland Games and Burns Suppers, which seem to constitute the main visible markers of ancestry (though I have also enjoyed encountering a Palestinian pipe band and a kilted Zimbabwean on my travels).

Many of these visits were an opportunity to learn in more depth and more detail about some of the legacies of British imperialism, mostly because they were being shared by the descendants of those whose forebears had experienced its dark underside, and who were still living with the consequences.

In 1999, I visited a First Nation reservation in Ontario, Canada. There, I met three generations of women of one family, and heard something of their story. The grandmother and granddaughter both had names in their own First Nation language, the mother had an English name. As a child, she had been removed from her family and nation and sent to a Canadian residential school, where every effort had been made to erase from her memory all traces of her tribal identity, language and culture, and to assimilate her into the dominant Anglo-Canadian society around her. These efforts had had mixed outcomes, and she spoke of feeling disconnected and alienated now from both cultures. She was also to a degree disconnected from both her mother and her teenage daughter; from the former because love was mixed with loss and ambivalence about the circumstances of her upbringing, from the latter because the young woman had rejected the assimilation forced on her mother and had identified strongly with her grandmother, learning, or relearning, the tribal language, customs and spiritual practices. This is not an uncommon story in Canada, but it was acutely painful to listen to.

The Truth and Reconciliation Commission of Canada, established to uncover the truth about these government-authorised schools, and the multiple abuses within them, described the practice as *'cultural genocide'*. The last school did not close until 1996. Most of them were run by Catholic or Anglican organisations. In 2008, the Canadian Prime Minister offered an official apology on behalf of the government of Canada. But Scotland has its own apologies to make.

In 2020, the Church of Scotland apologised for its role in sending children to Australia in the 1950s and '60s. The church said the aim was *'to give children a better opportunity for the future'*. But it now admits the programme was *'ill-conceived'* and caused trauma and suffering to many families:

'The Scottish Child Abuse Inquiry heard that the first migration ship linked to the church set sail in December 1950, with 22 boys aged under 14 on board.

'The scheme continued until 1963.

'Over this period, thousands of young British children were deported, with the help of charities and organisations across the UK.

'The children often came from deprived backgrounds and were

already in some form of care.

'*Many of the parents gave up their children because of poverty or the social stigma of being a single mother.*

'*Vivienne Dickson, chief executive of the religious organisation's Crossreach, told the inquiry that the Church of Scotland was pressured to get more child migrants sent to Australia to keep up with Catholics and other faiths.*

'*She said the "starting point" was to gain consent from each boy, although the known age range of the children involved started at seven.*

"*I would not believe a child of seven could give that informed consent," she said.*

'*The inquiry heard that the General Assembly of the Church of Scotland gave its backing to the scheme at its 1951 meeting.*

'*Inquiry chairwoman Lady Smith said this would have "put quite some pressure" on its members to ratify – as it had already begun the year before.*

'*All of those who left for Australia with the church ended up at Dhurringile in Victoria, which became a training farm for the youngsters … although the aim was to give the children a better future, the church now acknowledged that this was not what happened.*'[8]

In 2004, I took part in an international pilgrimage of about 600 people to Elmina Castle (in reality, a military garrison fortress built by the Portuguese then held by the Dutch and the British in turn) on the coast of Ghana, that held those who had been abducted and captured into slavery, as they suffered in dungeons waiting for slave ships that would take them to unknown lands and destinies. Over four brutal centuries, 15 million African slaves were transported to the Americas, and millions more were captured and died. On this trade in humans as commodities, wealth in Europe was built. Through their labour, sweat, suffering, intelligence and creativity, the wealth of the Americas was developed.

At the Elmina Castle, the Dutch merchants, soldiers, and Governor lived on the upper level, while the slaves were held in captivity one level below. We entered a room that had been used as a church, with words from Psalm 132 on a sign still hanging above the door ('For the Lord has chosen Zion ...'). And we imagined Christians worshipping their God while directly below them, right under their feet, those being sold into slavery languished in the chains and unimaginable horror of those dungeons. For the more than four centuries of European occupation of Elmina, this awful travesty went on.

Some of us who were there were descendants of those who were enslaved – African Americans from North America, from the Caribbean, from South America. Others of us were descended from those slave traders and slave owners, if not directly, then as citizens of European countries which were hugely complicit in it. We were confronted with the extent to which this commodification of human beings had profited or impoverished our own countries. We had been shamed that all of this had been done by professing Christians, and been forced to consider the extent of our own complicity in the continuing dehumanising effects of globalised markets, debt bondage, trade injustice and environmental degradation. In our rituals, we shared responses of tears, silence, anger, and lamentation. The dance was sombre and anguished, the drums sobbed.

I think now that the pilgrimage to Elmina reflected the kind of inner as well as outer journeys that I had been making for years. I have had the opportunity to see the world through the eyes of those who live in it unprotected by wealth, power, status or any of the myriad insurances we have to defend ourselves from what is reality for most people. What they had shown me so often was the power of hope in the midst of suffering and the absolute value of human kindness.

I have had the opportunity to see my society through the eyes of the world, and put Western whingeing and mean-spiritedness in a clearer, and not always flattering, perspective. Are we like over-indulged children, prone to tantrums if we don't get our own way (which we sometimes confuse with freedom), good at making messes but not so good at cleaning up after us? Often. My experience has meant that, practically every day, I am grateful to be able to turn on a tap in my house, and have clean water come out.

Thinking back over all these lives of the ancestors – their struggles and the fears they must have felt, the huge problems and challenges they faced, their profound sorrows and losses – I also see their courage, their commitment (even when it was to things that now seem to have been wrong), their persistence and their wisdom, their strength and their achievements. They were shaped by their families, communities and cultures, as I am. But most of all, I can't help thinking that the stories from this ordinary family from the north-west corner of Europe demonstrate how connected the world is.

Notes:

1.   From 'The Irish famine', by Jim Donnelly:
     www.bbc.co.uk/history/british/victorians/famine_01.shtml

2.   ibid.1

3.   Marlene NourbeSe Philip, from *She Tries Her Tongue; Her Silence Softly Breaks*, Poui Publications. (Edict I and Edict II from 'Discourse on the Logic of Language'; 'When the smallest cell …', from Universal Grammar; 'absencelosstears …' from She Tries Her Tongue; Her Silence Softly Breaks; 'Hold we to the centre …', from She Tries Her Tongue; Her Silence Softly Breaks.) Used by permission of M. NourbeSe Philip, www.nourbese.com

4.   The *Dundee Courier & Advertiser*, 26th September, 1929

5.   ibid. 4

6.   ibid. 4

7.   ibid. 4

8.   From 'Church of Scotland says sorry over child migrants', 2 October, 2020:
      www.bbc.co.uk/news/uk-scotland-54387212

Who are we?

*'Nations and peoples are largely the stories they feed themselves.
If they tell themselves stories that are lies, they will suffer the
future consequences of those lies. If they tell themselves stories
that face their own truths, they will free their histories for future
flowerings.'*

(Ben Okri, *Birds of Heaven*)[1]

When she was a child, about eight years old, my daughter used to
irritate her older brothers by repeatedly asking them 'what is the
meaning of life?' One of them was too busy living to be bothered
with such trivial questions; the other, of a slightly more philosophical bent, informed her that the meaning of life was to discover the
meaning of life. She found neither of these responses entirely satisfactory, and a few years later embarked on an enormously long
period of study to become a clinical psychologist, in which role she
now accompanies others struggling with this question.

In exploring, or imagining, the lives of one's ancestors, this is
equally a challenging question. 'What is the meaning of this life?'
needs a better answer than simply, 'because it gave me my life',
though that fact is undeniably true. Probably a more accessible question is to ask what gave meaning to *their* lives, what mattered to
them, what was significant? And how will I know or recognise that
from the vast amount of documentation we now have about them,
given from the infinitely greater amount that we do not have.

We know the basic facts of their lives: where and when and to
whom each of them was born; where and how they lived, worked
and supported themselves economically; who they married and
what children they had; when, and from what cause, did they die.
Looking back through the preceding chapters from the perspective
of the 21st century, several salient points strike me.

Almost all of them came from large families, and had large families in their turn. Simply providing for and raising their children

must have been, and was, very hard work and very time-consuming. Until the advent of the welfare state, they were the primary means of support for each other in times of crisis or unemployment, especially the poorer ones. But their family lives also had to contend with migration of some members to places so far away that the likelihood of ever meeting again was small. Their health was much more at risk, far more of them died in childbirth or in infancy, and their life expectancy was years, even decades, less than mine is. Many of them lived in bad housing conditions and did unpleasant and sometimes dangerous work. From my comfortable 21st-century perspective, their daily existence appears unimaginably hard.

Periodically, their lives were touched by war, but though James Orr and Adam Campbell both served in France, having been called up as reservists towards the end of the First World War, the only record we have of a family member's death in that war was Alexander Morrin, grandson of Maurice and Sarah, who died in Shakespeare Street Military Hospital, Glasgow, in 1919, from injuries sustained at Gallipoli. The terrible ordeal and death suffered by our uncle Bertie Orr in Malaya in 1942 was the only Second World War fatality in our close family.

Family members also had brushes with the criminal justice system: my maternal great-grandfather, Thomas Thomson, spent some time in the early 1870s in a reformatory school (what we would now call a young offenders institution) where he was learning to be a baker in the pursuit of his reformation. And in 1912, my maternal great-great-uncle by marriage, Gavin Paton, was tried at the High Court of Justiciary in Edinburgh, along with seven other miners, for mobbing and rioting at Tarbrax, a small village in South Lanarkshire where there was a shale mine. This incident was part of the first national miners' strike in the UK, whose goal was to secure a national minimum wage, in which, after 37 days, they were successful when the government passed the Coal Mines (Minimum Wage) Act. The case against Gavin was found to be not proven. Both of these brushes with the law seem to me to be more indicative of the exigencies of poverty than of any deep-seated criminality. Over three centuries, our family in its different branches seems to have been generally law-abiding.

In the mining side of the family, at least in the early 20th century, much energy, and presumably much of what free time there was from long hours down the pits, seems to have been given to the dramatic arts. For many years after World War I, my grandfather Clement Johnston was a leading light and driving force in the Stoneyburn Amateur Dramatic Club, whose productions were extensively reported on and reviewed in the *Midlothian Advertiser* in the 1920s. Clement was the stage manager (effectively the director) and played leading roles in a series of plays bearing eye-catching titles: *Waiting for the Verdict, The Face at the Window, Girl of My Heart*, all of which were highly melodramatic, and sometimes quite ghoulish murder mysteries. The Johnstons had wider family involvement too: my grandmother Sarah was the musical director, and in one play, ten-year-old Lizzie, their daughter, performed a speciality song and dance routine. Community drama groups were common in coal mining communities; the Fife miner, Joe Corrie, was known for his radical, working-class plays, and I remember my mother producing his *In Time of Strife* when she in her turn became an able and enthusiastic producer of community plays and musical revues in St John's Church, Oxgangs.

The creative impetus has continued down through the generations as families have become more financially stable and arts education, for the post-war fifty years at least, more accessible, producing not only many enthusiastic choir singers but also several writers, two professional ballet teachers, two artists, an award-winning documentary filmmaker and an award-winning actor.

Sport too has been a consistent preoccupation of my family since at least the late 19th century. Athletics, tennis, swimming, rugby, golf, rowing, volleyball have all been pursued, sometimes to a representative standard. But undoubtedly it has been football which has attracted the most fervent devotion, both playing it (producing one professional footballer) and supporting it, for at least a century. And although I am one of the few members of my family not to share this passion, and to have never attended a football match, I can at least claim the distinction of having written a foreword to a book about a Scottish football club, for which the other foreword was written by the distinguished Scottish manager of Manchester United in their glory years, Sir Alex Ferguson.

The arts and sport certainly provided recreation, enjoyment and community in the midst of hard lives. In that, they were like most Scots. But it's probably accurate to say that for the most part of the last three hundred years, and before the advent of higher education for any of them, meaning in life for our ancestors was hugely shaped by the church. For at least some of them, this seems to have been based on genuine conviction and interest, rather than the socially-expected adherence to the givenness of the intellectual air they breathed; that is to say, their adherence was voluntary as well as involuntary. Andrew Campbell, buying weighty theological books in 1751, displays a religious literacy and literary connectedness unusual for its time, especially in an Ayrshire farmer. And the landscape gardener John Fleming, in his 1880 Introduction to *Wild Flowers of the West of Scotland*, is as eloquent about theology as he is about botany.

For at least 150 years, the church was the centre of community life, social activity and cultural expression for my family, as it was for so many. It was also a professional vocation to an unusual degree. Of all the currents that have flowed together to create our story, this is probably the one in which it's possible to see the greatest continuity through the generations. It's also possible to read the ripple of dissent and the impetus for change from early on, even though it took different forms at different times. Perhaps this is a particularly geographical phenomenon. At the end of the 15th century, well before the Covenanters or even the Great Debate at Maybole during the Scottish Reformation, a group of Scottish followers of the English theologian John Wycliffe were sent for trial for heresy before King James IV, though the charges were dismissed. Wycliffe sought reform of the church, and the right of people to read the Bible and worship in their own language. They became known as the Lollards (the pejorative term used for Wycliffe's followers) of Kyle, the Ayrshire area they came from. Interestingly, to us at any rate, members of Clan Campbell were linked to Lollardy and Protestantism from the start with the Campbells of Cessnock caught up in the heresy trial. The tradition of religious dissent remained very strong among the Ayrshire Campbells who were involved in iconoclasm and supporting George Wishart's preaching campaign in the 1530s and 1540s. The south-west of Scotland has always been a home of dissent.

I have written in an earlier chapter about the positive and creative expressions of Christian church life I have experienced, and about the role it played in shaping my own values, and those of other family members, including the ones who no longer affiliate to any church. However, I recognise that this way of being church is passing away. The Christian story, for most people in Scotland, and particularly for younger Scots, is no longer a story to live by. In a secular society, where churchgoing is no longer socially or culturally mandated, God as explanation is meaningless, or irrelevant; God as a supernatural legal system dispensing punishment and reward according to variously defined obscure criteria has a long and fear-filled history in Scotland, which has been by and large glad to get rid of it. And many of the current manifestations of Christian belief across the world are unattractive, incomprehensible, reprehensible or just plain creepy. A deity whose name and scripture has been claimed at various times to support and legitimise pretty much anything, from gender inequality and sexual and minority violence to slavery, and from land claims to an imperial 'civilising' destiny, is not a story which speaks to young Scots today. The claims, privileges and power of the church have all but gone.

In 1997, our father Jack, who wrote hardly anything in his life except sermons, wrote this for the magazine of the Iona Community:

> '*So, then, spirituality describes for me: the attempt to live my daily life continually aware of God's presence in all His creation, in other people and in the world around me; trying to do my daily work and everyday tasks, whatever they may now be or ever were, in the Spirit of Jesus, in tolerance and goodwill and forgiveness offered; appreciation of nature in all its colour and wonder; knowing how much I fail and how greatly I need and receive forgiveness from God and my fellow human beings; knowing too how much I need the support of fellow human beings, Christian and non-Christian alike, and of the Church today, despite all its shortcomings (of which I am part).*'[2]

For both Jack and our mother Janet – teacher, singer, trade unionist, creative spirit – Christian faith was almost entirely relational, not institutional nor propositional. The local church to which they were dedicated was a community, not a temple. Their legacy was one of ground-breaking good work; of countless people encouraged and valued; of wisdom and kindness; of love and friendship. And though their children and grandchildren would mostly not call themselves Christian, they all share a deep respect for a lived faith which practised what it preached.

I think this is also so for many Scots now. Without feeling the need to accept the over-arching narrative of Christianity, they nevertheless value many aspects of Christian background or heritage, of care and service. It may not be their story to live by, but they find inspiration and encouragement in some of the multiple Christian stories, especially those of Jesus of Nazareth. They still love, are moved by and sometimes sing the songs of Christian spirituality. And the symbols of faith that have shaped us in the past, for good or ill, still shape us in ways we do not always recognise or understand;

especially perhaps in Scotland, the book, not necessarily the Bible per se, but that it stands for the value of literacy and education.

If the church was one important influence on my family over more than three centuries, a second major influence was that of the British Empire. Andrew Campbell, my six-times great-grandfather, was born 27 years before the Acts of Union in 1707. I find it curiously fascinating that I am directly connected, by generation and by the long process of remembering, to someone who lived to manhood while Scotland was still a sovereign state, and had been for at least five hundred years. The Union of Parliaments was almost exactly concurrent with the nascent trading empire that England was establishing, especially with its American colonies. The ill-fated Darien Scheme had put paid to any notion that The Company of Scotland Trading to Africa and the Indies could compete with the English East India Company. But now that trade tariffs with England had been removed as a consequence of the Union (and their removal was a major reason for the powerful men in the Scottish Parliament to vote in favour of union), Scotland's ability to trade freely with English colonies saw her economy grow massively, especially in the Lowlands, and created huge wealth for a new class of merchants.

In the 18th century, the weaving towns of Paisley and Kirkintilloch, the mining counties of West Lothian and Stirling, and above all, the city of Glasgow, were utterly transformed by colonial trade. Tobacco, sugar and cotton from the Americas, textiles and tea from India and China all made their way into the homes of Scottish people through the ports of Scotland and were beginning to be processed into manufactured goods and traded on across the world. Agriculture underwent its own revolution as the common lands were enclosed, and wage labour became increasingly common. Members of my family lived through all of these changes; some profited by them, others suffered because of them.

The wealth of this empire was greatly founded on conquest and the exploitation of other people's persons, lands, resources and natural and cultural heritage; what William Dalrymple, writing about the British East India Company, describes as *'state-sponsored corporate crime'*.[3] It is not possible to live in the city of Glasgow, even in 2021, without seeing the evidence of the criminal activity that was the slave trade, and especially plantation slavery, in the built environment, in the street names, in the many statues erected to famous men whose fortunes were founded on this criminal activity and the generals who were acclaimed for the slaughter of tens of thousands in India, Ireland, China, the West Indies (and not incidentally, for the deaths of the tens of thousands of hapless British soldiers who had no choice in the matter).

I do not share the opinion of those who believe we should not judge these men, 'because the times were different and so was the morality'. In the late 18th century, and again in the 1820s, tens of thousands of men and women wrote letters, signed petitions, held public meetings and campaigned for the ending of the transatlantic slave trade and then the ending of plantation slavery. They are witnesses to the fact that there were plenty of people in these times who adhered to a different morality, and said no, sometimes at great personal cost, to these iniquitous practices. Engaging in them, profiting by them, covering up for them and then trying to whitewash them was a choice. There was always an alternative. It is impossible to second-guess what the outcomes of such alternatives might have been; nevertheless, one can still wish that they had been pursued.

We have been surprised to discover the extent to which our family was impacted by slavery, even at the very humble social level that most of them occupied. Mostly that was by working as weavers, or servants to those who had made their money through their colonial businesses, or as sailors in merchant vessels, or as shopkeepers selling the new products, or as citizens visiting public landmarks and institutions. But that's how it happened all over Scotland, perhaps a better example of the 'trickle-down theory of wealth' than later ones. What cannot be ignored is the extent to which slavery and the slave trade, enriched then, and continue to enrich today, Scotland and the whole United Kingdom. And modern slavery, the trafficking of persons across the world as forced domestic, agricultural and sexual labour, is still a very present reality.

The 19th and early 20th centuries offered many opportunities for my family, members of whom took advantage of them in Canada, Australia, New Zealand, South Africa, the Gold Coast (now Ghana), India and Kenya. Interestingly, it was during the time between his ministries in New Zealand and Kenya that our great-uncle James Orr featured in a newspaper report in the *Dundee Courier* bearing the headline 'Barnhill's Patriotic Divine: A Champion of Scottish Ways'. This referred to a meeting of Dundee Presbytery, where the subject under discussion was the education of the ministry. James, then the minister of Barnhill Parish Church, took exception to the proposal that graduates of the University of London be admitted into Scottish Divinity Halls without first undergoing the normal required undergraduate study in a Scottish university. Though this might be an adequate test of scholarship, he felt that this would miss out on the spirit of community and sympathy fostered by such study (the University of London at that time was not itself a teaching university, but accredited degrees from a number of colleges). Furthermore, though he himself was a graduate of both a Scottish university and of London University, he felt that this exception gave a false notion of the value of English degrees as compared to Scottish degrees. James was adamant that nothing should appear to belittle Scottish degrees.

By this time, he was on a roll. '*The whole thing was of a piece with that insidious movement which was sapping the whole strength of our national life, running after English ways, English methods and English education, as if they were better than our own Scottish standards. There was a large section of the Scottish community which seemed to pride itself in belittling anything that belonged to their own nation. They sent their children to England to be educated because they were taught by*

English teachers, quite forgetting that we had in Scotland a system of education known throughout the world.[4] Though an imperialist to the core, James was always clear that Scotland should be recognised as an equal partner to England in the British Empire, and that 'nation' to him always meant Scotland. The headline writer in the *Dundee Courier* obviously agreed with him.

The West Lothian miners were as central to the workings of the Empire as its tea planters and civil servants and shopkeepers; their work powered the engines of production and transport, though they got less reward for their labours. It's in their generations underground that I can best see demonstrated the fate of those who possessed neither land nor capital (and many of the earliest mine owners were from the landed classes). This is not just about their terrible housing and working conditions, but about how little they had a voice, how limited were their opportunities to speak in their own interests. They did not have a vote, and few of the middle- and upper-class Members of Parliament could be relied on to advocate on their behalf. Community solidarity and eventually the trade union movement and the founding of the Independent Labour Party by a former coal miner, Keir Hardie, began to bring about change, and loyalty to the Labour movement and the foundation of the welfare state and the NHS kept my family firmly a Labour-voting one until the end of the 20th century.

All of the mothers and fathers, going back ten generations, who appear in this book, would probably find aspects of present-day Scotland almost incomprehensible. Dalrymple has probably changed the least; it's still a quiet East Ayrshire parish and village, surrounded by farmland, and the churchyard with its ancient Campbell graves. It's still beautiful and community-minded, and the Campbells of old would doubtless be delighted that the fame of their local hero Robert Burns is now worldwide and unassailable, and that he is considered to be Scotland's national poet. They might be more surprised that the local big house, Skeldon House, having been rebuilt in the 18th century as a fine Georgian mansion, had been sold for £2.5 million in 2020 by its most recent owner, an immensely rich Malaysian businessman, who owned both an airline company, AirAsia, and a famous London football club, Queen's Park Rangers.

The pits are all closed in the former mining villages of Polmont and Redding, Stoneyburn and Addiewell. All of them are now predominantly commuter villages, though they are also known for their nearby prisons. Kilcreggan, on the Rosneath Peninsula, is still beautiful, unspoiled and largely well-heeled. And Glasgow – well, the city has expanded its bounds greatly, but its population, which grew to rank it as one of the largest cities in Europe in 1900, its industrial peak, has now contracted from just over a million to 650,000, and the industries that made it great have all but gone. The salmon have come back to the River Clyde, so clean is it now.

The huge changes in the lives of women would probably be welcomed by the many strong women among our forebears. The franchise, freely available contraception, access to higher education, equality (at least theoretically and in law) with men across a comprehensive range of activities, welfare and work benefits in relation to maternity and childcare, a greatly increased access to job opportunities – all of these, and more, over the last seventy-five years, have made the lives of women unrecognisable in many regards. The social and cultural attitudes which so narrowly defined their status and value over the last three centuries have undergone huge shifts, which show up as much in the women's rugby teams and weightlifters who compete in sporting tournaments as in the women politicians and scientists who are now accepted without question in most quarters.

But the lives of women living in Scotland are still constrained by male violence in all its manifestations, and by class inequality. To look back over three hundred years and speculate about social change is to be confronted once more with Marx's question in the mid-19th century:

'Does it require deep intuition to comprehend that man's ideas, views, and conception, in one word, man's consciousness, changes with every change in the conditions of his material existence, in his social relations and in his social life?'[5]

Whatever meaning, belonging, identity meant to our ancestors in Scotland, and however their values were shaped in their own day, what have been transmitted to my siblings and myself are shared and strongly-held beliefs in justice, education and the common good, translated into public service, social activism and love of country. These values are not peculiar to Scotland or the other countries in the United Kingdom. They are found everywhere in the world. But in holding them, from our middle-class and working-class roots, we are characteristic of many people in Scotland, predominantly state-educated and not all having been born in Scotland, for whom the future of our country is a serious concern.

Being a country is first of all about place, geography, habitat. Scotland as a country predates the Act of Union, has survived and mostly thrived within the Union and I have no doubt that it will continue to exist as a country. It has the advantage of having had secure borders since 1482, when Berwick-upon-Tweed reverted to being part of England. Of course, this is not just about geography, it's also about institutions and diversity. Scotland has had different legal and educational systems, its own national media and different religious institutions since well before the devolution process instituted the Scottish Parliament in 1999. These institutions are not better or worse because they are Scottish; some are better than those elsewhere, some are worse and none of them are exempt from the need for constant scrutiny, review and change. They are simply different, and their difference arises from the particularities of its history, as differences do anywhere. Some of these are described in the preceding chapters.

So I don't, and won't, need a constitutionally independent

Scotland to be Scottish. Until 31st January 2020, I was also a citizen of the European Union and of the United Kingdom of Great Britain and Northern Ireland. This was my civic identity according to my passport. This identity has now been removed from me by the 2016 referendum on exiting the EU (Brexit), against my will and against the will of the majority of Scottish voters. The strong possibility of another referendum on Scotland's place in the United Kingdom in the next few years is what I must now consider anew, and Brexit will play a part in that consideration. This is not in my view an issue of nationalism, since any democratic self-determination will inevitably pose a variety of national choices; we cannot act as if *'your neigh-bour's nationalism is always toxic and xenophobic and your nationalism is always good'*.[6]

Any referendum will not be for me a matter of identity. Who we are is always a constellation of involuntary identities (such as gender, sexual orientation, ethnicity, class) and voluntary ones (such as religion, politics or profession) and even within these there is considerable fluidity. Nationality is only one marker of identity. I describe myself as Scottish, and Scotland as the country where I live and belong, and which I have a deep love for. This love is shared by many people of different ethnicities who were not born here but have chosen to make this country their home, and who also have a sense of belonging here.

Nor is it a matter of culture, as Ben Okri reminds me in the quote at the top of this chapter. There are plenty of stories – one might even call them myths – which Scots like to tell themselves: the myth of victimhood, the myth of Enlightenment, the myth of internation-alism, the myth of egalitarianism. Whatever the truth in them, and there is always some truth in myths, each of them has their deep shadow side, which makes them an unreliable basis on which to free our history for future flowering. Each creates its own exclusions, and we should do our best to deny the dead a mortgage on the living. The basis for my decision-making in any future referendum will therefore be a political one.

I have actively campaigned all my adult life for the abolition of nuclear weapons, and I would love to see the removal of Trident, not just from Scotland but from the UK and ultimately from everywhere. However, I have observed that political parties that support the removal of Trident while in opposition are often ready to abandon this when they get into government. It is possible that a categorical Scottish refusal to host Trident, and the subsequent choices that would need to be made by the remaining countries in the Union, would open up real alternative possibilities, especially if these nuclear-armed submarines were no longer located somewhere out of sight and therefore out of mind. I would like to think so, but I don't hold my breath about this; the impetus to retain Trident has nothing to do with defence and everything to do with the defence industry and even more with the UK's seat on the UN Security Council and its perennial imperial desire to be a big global player. The stakes are very high here. They have not been lowered in any way by the 2021 decision by the Conservative government to raise the cap on the number of Trident nuclear warheads it can stockpile by more than 40%, ending thirty years of gradual disarmament since the end of the Soviet Union. The amount of money spent on this process will be breathtaking, and will maintain Scotland's position as the most heavily-militarised country in Western Europe.

The democratic deficit (whereby Scotland, more definitely on the left, is likely, because of its smallness relative to England, to be governed within the United Kingdom by parties it did not elect) is also a growing political problem, especially for the Labour Party. The SNP victories in recent Scottish elections have shown an overwhelming rejection of Labour, even in its former Scottish heartlands. The United Kingdom is now (2021) in a situation where every one of its constituent parts is governed by a different political party: devolved government in Scotland by the SNP, in Wales by Labour, in Northern Ireland by an always fragile power-sharing executive

led by Sinn Féin and the Democratic Unionist Party (currently sus-
pended), England by the present UK Conservative government. Our
unreformed and increasingly archaic first-past-the-post voting
system, which leaves many citizens of the UK unrepresented, is
unlikely to change any time soon, and an extremely right-wing government, bolstered by a right-wing press, and receiving less than
50% of the popular vote even in England, seems secure for some
time to come.

This democratic deficit has been exacerbated by Brexit, which
has not only overridden the vote of people in Scotland and Northern
Ireland, but has put at grave risk the Good Friday Agreement of
1998. This had found a creative and innovative way to reconceptu-
alise citizenship within Northern Ireland, and enabled the charting
of a direction out of the violence that had caused the deaths of 3000
people during the thirty-year Troubles. The utterly divisive fact of
partition, and the long colonial history preceding it, finally seemed
as if it would not always be the last word about Northern Ireland.
That Brexit has so seriously destabilised the achievements of the
Good Friday Agreement is in my view unforgivable. That it did so
in such a cavalier fashion is shameful.

In the UK today, only one pillar of state is elected, the House of
Commons. The unelected House of Lords (the largest upper house
anywhere in the world), the monarchy, the proliferation of quangos
and public bodies, the outsourced state, the City of London, the
Crown Dependencies and Overseas Territories, many of them major
tax havens, the security state of NATO, Trident and the military-
industrial UK/US alliance, engaging in mass citizen surveillance, all
unelected, all democratically unaccountable, have served to
entrench a version of the UK centred on power, privilege, money
and its related institutions. This is not just about politics and economics; it is a culture of neo-liberalism as an all-pervasive social
order, which prioritises the individual as competitive, self-defining
and, under the guise of choice, as consumer, what Scottish writer

Tom Leonard memorably described as *'a bought behaviour pattern'*.[7]

People living in Scotland are constantly being invited to affirm that we are better together on the basis of how good the United Kingdom has been for Scotland. But that may not represent the view from everywhere. In the 19th century, systematic land clearance by landlords pushed the indigenous population into mass emigration and urbanisation. The destruction of Scotland's industrial base in the 1980s, driven by a ruthless pursuit of efficiency and profitability, led to a significant increase in the numbers living in poverty. I think it is not fanciful to say that this process was the urban equivalent to the Clearances. Only now there are no dominions to ship the redundant people off to.

And every day now, we are witness to the huge, preventable human suffering caused in the world's poorest countries by climate change, not as a theoretical future possibility, but as a present reality. I am ashamed every day by the lack of serious concerted vision and action by Western governments on a global injustice which we have profited from in the past, continue to profit by in the present, for which the consequences are being borne by the world's most vulnerable populations and which greatly increase the risk of conflict, resource wars and uprooted peoples. So my vote in the referendum will be cast for the option which seems to me to hold the greater prospect of the political will, practical policies and popular support to address this and other injustices. But whatever the outcome, I will not expect any political party or government to have all the answers. I will certainly not expect it from a political party which seems to have embarked on a bizarre quasi-re-creation of the British Empire as a cover for its own wealth and privilege.

I see that for over three hundred years the United Kingdom has been constelled round three overarching stories: the story of empire, the story of two world wars and the story of the welfare state and the National Health Service. I am unconvinced that these stories are still strong enough and vital enough in Scotland to sustain a fragmenting union and a partial democracy, and I see no other story at present with sufficient practical, intellectual and emotional heft to take their place.

In the five years since I began this writing task of remembering the past, there have been many opportunities to reflect on the fact that the present is what the past is doing now. In the 'Black Lives Matter' and the 'Me Too' movements, in Ireland and Palestine, even in the plight of the planet itself, we are punished, not for but by our sins. Or to put it another way, we are confronted by the consequences of our actions, and our inactions. Our mining forebears did not become rich through mining. They lived in squalid conditions, their work was dirty, dangerous and sometimes fatal, their health cruelly compromised by their occupation. The rights and rewards available to them for their labour, notwithstanding its essential value to their country and people, seem remarkably meagre. Nevertheless, their strong communities took pride in the importance of their work, often the only kind available to them to feed their families. They did not know then that they were contributing to the greatest threat to human life on earth, negatively impacting whole ecosystems and accelerating climate change. Like Job, they did not know what they did not know. In their ignorance lay their innocence. Our generation will not have that excuse.

Making the acquaintance of those people whose lives gave birth to ours has also been a thought-provoking and occasionally inspiring journey. We have discovered relatives whose existence was hitherto unknown, numerous scandals, some achievements and that, probably like half the population of Scotland, we are distantly related to Robert Burns. Our opinion of our great-great-grandfather, Adam McLellan, has undergone several revisions, and our pride in our grandmothers and great-grandmothers has been enhanced. What seemed like a long time, nearly 350 years, has become much shorter; we are *never wholly separate, only a part of the time we live in, and with others occupy*.[8]

Perhaps looking back is more a preoccupation of those who become aware that they have more time behind them than ahead of them; generations are long, but one generation is short. The last couple of years have seen prodigious unexpected loss in our country as it has been ravaged by a coronavirus pandemic. We have had our own great loss; my sister's husband, Peter Macdonald, a much-loved and inspirational minister, died suddenly and too soon. The younger generation of our family were all devoted to him; I think it was because he was so utterly present in the here and now, in his vitality, compassion and passion for life. This book is for them, when it's the right time, and for all the ones to come.

Notes:

1. *Birds of Heaven*, Copyright © Ben Okri 1995. Reproduced by permission of Ben Okri c/o Georgina Capel Associates Ltd., 29 Wardour Street, London, W1D 6PS

2. Jack Orr, in *This Is the Day: Readings and Meditations from the Iona Community*, ed. Neil Paynter, Wild Goose Publications, 2002

3. William Dalrymple, in *The Anarchy: The Relentless Rise of the East India Company*, Bloomsbury Publishing, 2019

4. From the *Dundee Courier*, December 6, 2017

5. Karl Marx and Friedrich Engels in *The Communist Manifesto*, 1848, Chapter 2

6. Andrew Marr, Edinburgh Book Festival, 16/8/13

7. Tom Leonard, in *Being a Human Being*, Object Permanence, 2006. Used by permission of the Tom Leonard Literary Estate

8. Tom Leonard, from 'Proem', by Tom Leonard, from *access to the silence*, etruscan books, 2004. Used by permission of the Tom Leonard Literary Estate

Appendix: On researching a family history

I am the youngest of four children. So was my father. He was 40 when I was born; his father was 39 when he was born. My mother was the penultimate child in a family of eight; her mother and father were 37 and 45 respectively when she was born. Unusually, for a 1960s child, my grandparents were all born well before the end of the 19th century. Three of them died long before I came along and I was only eight when the Gran I did know and love dearly died in 1971. The significance of this became apparent decades later when I realised very suddenly how ignorant I was about my ancestors, not just those obscured by the mists of time, but even those just two generations back.

That sudden realisation came immediately after our Mum died (Dad had died a couple of years earlier). As I rummaged through old photos and a few letters and documents, questions flooded my mind for the first time. What do I know of my heritage? Where did I come from? Who were my ancestors? I had surprisingly few answers: ministers, miners, maybe something about a shopkeeper. Dumbarton, West Calder, had someone mentioned Ayrshire? … Beyond my Mum, Dad and Gran, I knew nothing of anyone else whose existence had, in turn, given me life. I was shocked by my ignorance and immediately determined to rectify it.

This was in 2003. Happily, my newfound interest coincided with a proliferation of web-based genealogical resources and a surging interest in tracing one's family tree, some perhaps inspired by the BBC's new programme *Who Do You Think You Are?*. The Scottish Government website www.scotlandspeople.gov.uk had been launched in 2002 and it immediately became (and remains) my first port of call for researching anyone who lived in Scotland. The searchable databases contain church and statutory records of births, deaths and marriages and comprehensive census returns for every decade between 1841 and 1911. For a charge, original certificates can be viewed, downloaded and printed.

Birth, death and marriage certificates become available on Scotland's People after 100 years, 50 years and 75 years respectively, thus, almost immediately after discovering this fantastic resource and by virtue of their Victorian births, I was able to find the relevant records for my grandparents, including their marriage certificates, rich with information, including their parents' names. The small family tree I had drafted rapidly expanded. Marriage certificates led to birth certificates and census returns, and very quickly, whole families could be plotted. I ran out of space on my page. My sketched notes were transferred onto an Excel database and soon I was investigating which genealogy software was best for recording and displaying information systematically. I chose 'Family Historian', which has served the purpose well and continues to evolve.

Statutory certification was introduced in 1855. As is still the case today, facts were presented by a family member and certified by a registrar. The facts recorded are mainly accurate. Prior to 1855, records were kept by the church and often restricted to a name and a date. Spelling was inconsistent and the archive is not complete. The older the record, the more likely it is to be difficult to read or ambiguous. On the other hand, back into the 18th and 17th centuries, it is far more likely that people were born, lived and died in the same small location.

Helpfully, most Scots followed a common convention when naming children. First sons were named after their paternal grandfather, first daughters after maternal grandmothers. Second sons were named after maternal grandfathers, second daughters after paternal grandmothers. Third sons were named after their fathers and third daughters, their mothers. It was also common for children to be given the same name as older siblings who had died and for mother and grandmother maiden names to be given as middle names. Knowing this pattern can focus a search and help to confirm that a child was born to a particular family.

I enjoyed populating an extensive family tree with names, dates and places quickly, but the satisfaction in doing this was soon over-taken by deeper questions. Who were these people, where and how did they live, what were they, and the Scotland they lived in, like?

The 1861 census reveals two of my great-grandparents living in very different circumstances. Ten-year-old Maggie McLellan in Abbotsburn, a ten-roomed mansion with servants, and a few miles away, seven-year-old Thomas Thomson sharing a two-roomed ten-ement with his mother, four siblings and a lodger. Ten years later, he and his brother were 'guests' in the Glasgow Reformatory School. Other records held by Scotland's People, including valuation rolls, wills and Kirk Session documents, offer glimpses and sometimes deep insight into our ancestors' occupations, lives and loves (the minutes of Kirk Session meetings are dominated by accounts of illicit fornication).

Fifteen of my sixteen great-great-grandparents were born and lived entirely in Scotland, and over a period of several years, I even-tually identified all of them and a good number of their forebears going back as far as 1650. It was only when researching the six-teenth, Maurice Morrin, that I realised just how fortunate we Scot-tish genealogists are to have Scotland's People. We know something of Maurice's life in Scotland. His marriage to Marrion Gilchrist, a fellow Celt from Islay, their children and her tragic early death; his work as a coachman, colliery labourer and lodging-house keeper; his migration from Ireland to west Scotland and then to Lothian. About Maurice in Ireland, despite hours of painstaking research, I can find nothing. A fire in the Dublin public records office in 1922 destroyed many records, including those from the 1841 and 1851 census (which would have been crucial). There are some good Irish sites, but I haven't found Maurice anywhere!

As my research followed family out of Scotland and around the world, www.ancestry.co.uk became my key resource. An annual subscription allows unlimited access to over thirty billion records. For me, those from England and North America have been invaluable, as have military records and ship passenger lists. More recently, I have also subscribed to www.findmypast.co.uk. It holds many of the same records as Ancestry, but also gives access to a massive, ever-expanding archive of local, national and international newspapers. Searching this database successfully requires some skill and considerable patience, especially if the person you seek has a common name, but newspaper articles, family notices and adverts can reveal facts and details which have been buried, in some cases for hundreds of years.

The National Library of Scotland has a wonderful free digital platform. Their vast selection of Scottish Post Office Directories covering two hundred years from 1773 is a great way to find out where people were living and working, while the sophisticated historical maps section pinpoints exact locations, many of which have since been lost, for example Woodmuir, birthplace of our grandmother, Sarah.

While the vast depth and searchability of online resources is brilliant, more traditional research methods are still invaluable. Whenever I visit a place with a family connection, I try to visit the local cemetery and library. Standing at a grave, imagining ancestors gathered in that place for a family funeral, reduces the aeons between us and can conjure strong emotions. Headstones sometimes convey personal words never seen on a death certificate and who knows what gems might be found in the library. Even when such visits fail to yield anything specific to family research, one's understanding of the social history and sense of a place is invariably enhanced.

Tracing ancestors is interesting and rewarding. It can also be poignant, uncomfortable and painful. I was shocked to learn from her death certificate that Catherine Lyall McLellan died in 'Glengall Lunatic Asylum' near Ayr in 1872. The building is still there, now part of Ailsa Hospital. A speculative e-mail to the records department and helpful reply confirmed that Catherine had been a patient there for just over a month before her death. Later I was able to visit the Ayrshire records archive and read the entries made about Catherine in that last month, which are covered in the chapter 'A mid-Victorian family, 1822-1891'.

Family history societies are full of helpful people with similar passions and access to local knowledge and resources. Most publish newsletters and organise talks and events.

Even with the incredible resources available to the 21st-century genealogist, there are many pitfalls, blind alleys and false hopes. In their eagerness to build a comprehensive tree, people can be careless. Both Ancestry and Find My Past allow subscribers to upload their own family trees and share them with other users. I often come across trees containing erroneous information and I learned early on not to trust someone else's information without doing my own authenticity checks. I aim to cross-reference between birth, marriage and death certificates, census information and any other information available before adding a new person to my tree. Today, my family tree has 1655 people, all related to me directly or by marriage. The tree will continue to grow as relationships are formed and new babies are born; as new data is made available allowing us to delve even further back in history; and as I discover new 2nd, 3rd, 4th … cousins. This has been facilitated by the explosion of DNA testing. The test I have taken confirmed what I already knew from my research. I share 84% of my DNA with people from Lowland Scotland and 12% with people from Ireland. The final 4% is split equally between Scandinavia and Wales – presumably further back in time and perhaps never to be confirmed by written records. Having tested and shared my DNA profile through Ancestry, I can browse a list of 25,000 (yes 25,000!) people to whom I am distantly related. Thankfully, the list is sorted with the closest relatives first and through this, I have been in contact with several newly discovered cousins.

Typically, the first (excellent) advice given to someone starting to research their family history is to talk to family members. I am grateful to siblings and cousins who have shared pictures, documents, first-hand family memories, legends and perhaps a few myths. Sadly, my opportunity to quiz past generations had been lost many years earlier and I so regret that I only embarked on this journey after my parents died. How I would have loved to discuss my findings with them!

Callum Orr

Bibliography

In addition to the books and websites cited in the chapter notes, I read widely on Scottish history over the last 350 years. The following were particularly helpful.

Additional reading:

David Alston, *Slaves and Highlanders: Silenced Histories of Scotland and the Caribbean*, Edinburgh University Press, 2021

Judith Bowers, *Glasgow's Lost Theatre: The Story of the Britannia Music Hall*, Birlinn, 2014

Callum G Brown, *Religion and Society in Scotland since 1707*, Edinburgh University Press, 1997

T M Devine, *The Scottish Clearances: A History of the Dispossessed*, Penguin, 2018

T M Devine, *The Scottish Nation, 1700-2000*, Allen Lane, The Penguin Press, 1999

Ron Ferguson, *George MacLeod: Founder of the Iona Community*, Wild Goose Publications, 2001

W Hamish Fraser & R J Morris (Eds.), *People and Society in Scotland, Vol II, 1830-1914*, John Donald, 1990

Catriona M M Macdonald, *Whaur Extremes Meet: Scotland's Twentieth Century*, John Donald, 2009

Alex Matheson, *Glasgow's Other River: Exploring the Kelvin*, Fort Publishing, 2000

Jonathan Moffatt & Audrey Holmes McCormick, *Moon over Malaya: A Tale of Argylls and Marines*, Coombe Publishing, 1999

Andy Wightman, *The Poor Had No Lawyers: Who Owns Scotland (And How They Got It)*, Birlinn Ltd, 2013

Additional website reading:

https://glasgowwestindies.wordpress.com (A Glasgow-West India Sojourn | Ponderings of a Glasgow Historian of the Caribbean)

www.addiewellheritage.org.uk

www.artisansinscotland.wordpress.com

www.canmore.org.uk (National Record of the Historical Environment)

www.crawfordjohn.org

www.drmarkjardine.wordpress.com (Jardine's Book of Martyrs)

www.findmypast.co.uk

www.genuki.org.uk

www.gla.ac.uk (University of Glasgow)

www.scottishmining.co.uk (Scottish Mining website)

www.scottishshale.co.uk (Museum of the Scottish Shale Oil Industry website)

www.theguardian.com

www.ucl.ac.uk/lbs (Centre for the Study of the Legacies of British Slavery)

www.visionofbritain.org.uk

www.wikipedia.org